Preservation of the Truth

Joseph D. Small

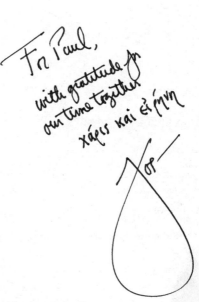

For Paul,
with gratitude for
our time together
χάρις καὶ εἰρήνη

Witherspoon Press
Louisville, Kentucky

Witherspoon Press gratefully acknowledges the support of the Offices of the General Assembly and Theology and Worship for the publication of *Preservation of the Truth*.

Publisher: Sandra Albritton Moak
Editor: Martha Gilliss

First edition

Published by Witherspoon Press
Louisville, Kentucky

Web site address: www.pcusa.org/witherspoon

PRINTED IN THE UNITED STATES OF AMERICA

05 06 07 08 09 10 11 12 13 14—10 9 8 7 6 5 4 3 2 1

Library of Congress Cataloging-in-Publication Data

Small, Joseph D.
    Preservation of the truth/Joe Small.—1st ed.
        p. cm.

Includes bibliographical references.
    ISBN 1-57153-053-3
    1. Truth—Religious aspects—Christianity. I. Title.
    BT50.S62 2004
    230'.51—dc22   200402126

For my mother and father, with gratitude
Dalen S. Small †1995
Joseph D. Small, Jr.

Contents

Preface

Theology is a disagreeable word in the church, not only because people disagree about theology, but because theology is often thought to be unpleasantly abstract, abstruse musing that has little to do with the real life of people and churches. *Theologian* has become an angular word reserved for academic practitioners of an arcane skill, certainly not a description of pastors and church members.

Yet theology is never absent from the church. As we worship we pray, sing, listen to sermons or preach them, celebrate sacraments, share money, and greet others. We also come together in church committee meetings, study groups, and mission projects. These and other church activities combine with our experiences of family, job, friends, and events to make us think and talk about the presence (or absence) of God in our world and in our lives. Thinking and talking about God and God's Way in the world is the work of theology, and so there is a sense in which we are all theologians.

We may be very bad theologians, of course, and our theology may have more to do with our desires and dispositions than with God. Yes, all Christians are engaged in theological thinking and speaking, but Christian thoughts and words may be simpleminded, wrongheaded, unrealistic, and even dangerous. Even though all of us who think and talk about God are "theologians," most of us devote little time and effort to our calling. All too often, this results in the kind of careless, naive, and irregular thinking that is no more appropriate in the church than in business or government, no more acceptable in theology than in sociology or economics.

As Christ's disciples, we are called to serious, sustained thinking and talking together about God and God's Way in the world. We are called to seek God's truth attentively, to explore God's truth comprehensively, and live God's truth faithfully. None of this is easy. Theology is hard work, demanding time and effort. Theology, like other worthwhile pursuits, requires more from us than casual inattention. Our common calling to serious, sustained theological work is important for each of us individually, because it enables us to receive, appreciate, and live the abundant life God gives. It is also important for the church, because when theology is neglected the church tends to wander aimlessly, easily seduced by cultural notions of institutional worth.

It is my hope that this little book will be an occasion for serious, sustained theological exploration in the church. I do not presume that it is the whole truth about the preservation of the truth, but I have some confidence that the issues it raises can help persons and groups in the church inquire more deeply into the truth of the gospel and the urgent necessity of preserving this truth for the generations of Christians who will follow us. I also have confidence in the capacity of congregations to undertake the hard theological work that leads to deepened faith and broadened faithfulness.

My own thinking about the faith has always taken place in the company of others, especially with congregations and communities of colleagues. I have served as a pastor in the Towson (Maryland) Presbyterian Church, The First Presbyterian Church of Westerville, Ohio, and the Twelve Corners Presbyterian Church in suburban Rochester, New York. The saints in these congregations attended faithfully to my preaching and teaching, but they were my theological teachers and colleagues as well. These churches helped me become the kind of theologian that ministers are called to be, because they were the theological communities that congregations are called to be.

My theological work has developed and deepened through conversations with friends and colleagues in the Office of Theology and Worship of the Presbyterian Church (U.S.A.). Over the years, this remarkable group of theologians and liturgists has widened and sharpened my vision, enabling me to see essential things that I might not have noticed on my own, and would not have understood as well. My appreciation extends to wonderful ecumenical colleagues in the Faith and Order Commissions of the World Council of Churches and the National Council of Churches, and in the Theology Department of the World Alliance of Reformed Churches. I am also indebted to countless pastors throughout the church, especially those who have joined me in practicing the disciplines of the Company of Pastors.

I am grateful beyond measure to my wife, Valerie—a Presbyterian elder, assistant stated clerk of the General Assembly, and keen interpreter of Scripture. Daily, her energy, intelligence, imagination, and love present me with theological insight and personal joy. But more, she is the one "To whom I owe the leaping delight . . ."

All of these and many others are my teachers, colleagues, friends, and companions in a common quest to preserve the truth of the gospel.

Louisville
The Resurrection of the Lord, 2004

Introduction

Mission statements, vision statements, mission work plans: the church is awash in them. Congregations, governing bodies, and church institutions spend an inordinate amount of time preparing generalized statements of what they are to be and do. Unfortunately, church mission statements often bear a disturbing resemblance to the mission statements of grocery stores and pharmaceutical companies, employing marketing language to stress quality products and friendly service. Perhaps that is why they are so easily forgotten.

The churchly effort spent on devising mission statements would be better directed to a brief section in the first chapter of the Presbyterian Church (U.S.A.)'s *Book of Order*. Embedded in the church's preliminary principles (G-1.0200) is a short list of the "Great Ends of the Church." These six great purposes of the church's life—the life of every congregation and the whole denomination—express direction for mission with a clarity and substance that is rarely found in the isolated, temporary products of church committees. The Great Ends of the Church are

- the proclamation of the gospel for the salvation of humankind;
- the shelter, nurture, and spiritual fellowship of the children of God;
- the maintenance of divine worship;
- the preservation of the truth;
- the promotion of social righteousness; and
- the exhibition of the Kingdom of Heaven to the world.

The church's constitution presents us with six great aims to direct our life together, six basic works of the church that are foundational to who the church is and what the church is called to do.

Nearly a century old, this statement of the Great Ends of the Church was developed by the United Presbyterian Church of North America between 1904 and 1910. The Great Ends were preserved in the church's constitution when the United Presbyterian Church of North America united with the Presbyterian Church in the United States of America in 1958, and then again when this combined body, the United Presbyterian Church in the United States of America, was reunited with the Presbyterian Church in the United States in 1983 to form the Presbyterian Church (U.S.A.). The endurance of this little testimony from a small predecessor church is evidence of the Great Ends' capacity to inspire faith and faithfulness.

The Great Ends of the Church is not a list of disconnected items, but a holistic vision of the church's life. A church cannot be faithful to the intention of the Great Ends by choosing to emphasize proclamation of the gospel to the neglect of worship, or to guard the truth of Christian doctrine while ignoring social righteousness. The great purposes of the church are intimately related to one another, and none can be fully understood apart from the whole. Their interrelationship is shown in an interesting way if we pair them from the outside in:

- the proclamation of the gospel for the salvation of humankind *and* the exhibition of the Kingdom of Heaven to the world
- the shelter, nurture, and spiritual fellowship of the children of God *and* the promotion of social righteousness
- the maintenance of divine worship *and* the preservation of the truth

Note how these pairings break through some of the partitions that mar the church's landscape. No evangelism apart from demonstrating life within God's rule and no living the gospel without proclaiming the gospel. No care for ourselves without care for the world and no justice apart from personal relationships. No worship that neglects truth and no theology without praise and prayer. None of the Great Ends is independent of the others, and each depends on the others.

This book deals with only one of the Great Ends of the Church, "the preservation of the truth," but it is one in a series of six books exploring all of the Great Ends. Each of the books will be better appreciated when read together with the other five. All of the books will be appreciated more fully when read together with other people. Because the books are about the great ends of the *church*, church-centered reading enables individuals and groups to explore the implications of the Great Ends for congregational, governing body, and denominational life.

A few comments about language may be helpful to readers. The English language has developed in ways that sometimes express gender exclusivity, employing masculine nouns and pronouns to refer to all people. The Presbyterian Church (U.S.A.) recognizes this problem and acknowledges that the diversity present in both church and world is not always reflected in the language of the church. "Definitions and Guidelines on Inclusive Language," adopted by the 197th General Assembly (1984) and reaffirmed by the 212th General Assembly (2000), provides guidance that can help the church overcome the linguistic limitations embedded in English-language expressions of the Christian tradition.

The church's policy is clear that every effort should be made to use inclusive language with respect to the people of God. In fact, inclusive language for the people of God is no longer controvertible in most of the Presbyterian Church (U.S.A.). The church's clear commitment has even helped us to understand that the original inclusivity of some biblical, creedal, and liturgical texts has been masked by gender-exclusive English translations! As with everything that I write, this book attempts to be gender inclusive in every reference to God's people.

Language for God presents a more difficult problem. "Definitions and Guidelines" is clear that our language for God should be as intentionally diverse and varied as that of Scripture and tradition. Thus, we may use the full range of designations for God. "Definitions and Guidelines" is also clear that the Trinitarian designation "Father-Son-Spirit" is not to be altered, although it may be supplemented. (I say more about Trinitarian language in chapter 3.) The problem of language for God becomes particularly difficult with pronouns, however. The English options are *he*, *she*, and *it*. Use of *it* and *itself* to refer to God would be inappropriately impersonal, so we are left with a choice between masculine and feminine pronouns. "Definitions and Guidelines" recognizes the difficulty, suggesting the use of nouns rather than pronouns, for example "God shows God's love" rather than "God shows his love." Some writers substitute passive for active voice, as in "God's love is shown." Others eliminate the pronoun: "God shows love."

The English language does not lend itself to natural solutions. The church's legitimate concern for inclusive language sometimes has the unintended consequence of depersonalizing our talk about God and each other. Plural nouns, passive verbs, and neutral pronouns abound while gendered images are banished. While exclusive or predominant use of male terms is clearly inappropriate, inclusive language should be just that—inclusive—not excluding all hint of gender. This is particularly true when everyone realizes that linguistic conventions do not imply the belief that God is a male being.

I confess that I do not know a good solution, particularly in the case of pronouns. I have tried to work around the limitations of English grammar and syntax, but there are times, especially when indicating God's active engagement in the world, when the use of masculine pronouns seems unavoidable. At those points I can only trust we all know that God is beyond gender. God is neither male nor female, but rather the One who declares, "I am God and no mortal, the Holy One in your midst" (Hos. 11:9).

What Is Truth?

1

To know all is to see all, and omniscience is God's alone. I
state the obvious, I suppose, for if God exists, so does truth
and if there was no God (a thing not to be imagined in
seriousness, but a philosophical jest alone), then would truth
disappear from the world, and the opinion of one would be
no better than that of another. I might also reverse the
theorem, and say that, if men come to think that all is merely
opinion, then they must come to atheism as well.

—Iain Pears, *An Instance of the Fingerpost*[1]

The last week of Jesus' life passes before us in a blur of rapidly
changing events and shifting emotions. The days race from the odd
celebration of Jesus' entry into Jerusalem, to a near riot in the Temple,
ominous teachings, a farewell meal with disciples, a night in the
garden, betrayal, arrest, trial, execution . . . and then, improbably,
resurrection to new life. Yet in the midst of an unseemly stampede to
Golgotha some scenes unfold at a more measured pace. The
evangelists pause to narrate a few moments in reverent detail, so that
they almost appear to creep forward in slow motion.

Jesus' appearance before the Roman governor Pontius Pilate is a
scene of unusual poignancy (see John 18:28—19:16). Jesus of Nazareth,
so recently hailed by adoring crowds, now stands accused before the
power of Rome. He has been betrayed by one of his disciples, denied
by another, and abandoned by all of them. He has been rejected by
religious authorities and shuttled off to undergo judgment by political
powers. Now he undergoes a petty interrogation by a provincial official,
providing enigmatic responses to an exasperated Pilate.

The religious leaders have done all they can do. While they are
able to arrest and accuse and even punish, they have no authority to

execute. So, early in the morning, they hand Jesus over to the Roman governor. Pilate asks Jesus how he pleads to charges of blasphemy and sedition: "Are you the king of the Jews?" Jesus responds obliquely, asking if the accusation is Pilate's own or if it comes from others. The governor makes it clear that Jesus' own people have brought the charges, and that what he wants is a plea—guilty or not guilty? Again Jesus replies unsatisfactorily, "My kingship is not from this world." Grasping at whatever he can, Pilate takes this as an admission: "So you are a king?" Jesus dismisses Pilate with a brief "So you say," before stating what he wants to declare: "For this I was born, and for this I came into the world, to testify to the truth. Everyone who belongs to the truth listens to my voice." Then Pilate utters the words we remember him by: "What is truth?"

Does Pilate ask the question cynically? hopefully? dismissively? curiously? We don't know. Perhaps we do not even know how *we* intend the question when it passes through our minds. In an extended meditation on this scene, novelist Frederick Buechner imagines that Pilate asks the question ". . . because in a world of many truths and half truths, he is hungry for truth itself or, failing that, at least for the truth that there is no truth. We are all of us Pilate in our asking after the truth. . . ."[2] Buechner may be right. There are times when we know the discomfort of living in a world of half-truths and too many truths, times when we want so much to find the firm ground of truth on which to stand. But perhaps Buechner is too optimistic. We may not even bother to ask Pilate's question because we have become resigned to the suspicion that, in a world of half-truths and too many truths, there is no real truth to be had, and so no reason to ask after it.

Truth and Truths

Our culture is strangely ambivalent about truth. On the one hand we take it for granted that there are indisputable truths, facts that can be proven beyond doubt by the use of scientific method: our planet is round not flat, cigarette smoking increases the risk of disease, there is good cholesterol as well as bad, $E = mc^2$, and more. We live much of our lives in the confident belief that truths about the natural order of the physical world can be known, and that we can rely on those truths in the decisions we make. Perhaps more important, we can go though our days without having to think about these truths; we simply assume them. We do not have to decide about everything all the time.

Death and taxes are not the only certainties. Everyday life is lived in taken-for-granted certainty about "the way things are." We do not have to think about everything all the time because almost everything is simply *there*, self-evidently real. The truth about everyday life is that it is full of truths we accept without having to be conscious of them, much less prove them. Day follows night, household appliances work, plants need water, transportation systems get us to our destinations, eating too much food will cause us to gain weight, computers operate, moderate exercise is good for us, and CD players function. Life is not perfect, of course, so there are times when things "go wrong." But even then we are confident that they can be fixed. Moreover, we are confident that knowledge about the way things are will lead to improvements so that things will get even better. There is an order to everyday life and an order to problem solving in everyday life. Our culture assumes that there is truth about many things, and that this is truth we can count on daily.

Yet our culture also supposes that there are things about which there is no truth. Most dramatically, the culture assumes that there is no true social or moral order, or that there are many different but equally true social and moral orders. It seems that beyond the everyday arena of scientifically provable technological certainty there is a confusing maze of conflicting preferences. Whatever "truths" exist appear to be nothing more than relative, personal points of view. No one perspective is true while others are false. All are true in their own way, and so all must be respected.

This commonplace assumption that "truth" is a matter of perspective and preference also encompasses much of our everyday lives.

- I know that asparagus is delicious, while my son knows that asparagus is revolting. I am sure that Haydn is superior to twentieth-century composers, while my wife is certain that Rachmaninoff's music is far more elegant. Are these only matters of taste, with no standard of truth to decide who is right and who is wrong?

- I am committed to public education, while others are certain that private school education or home schooling is better for children. I almost always vote for Democrats, while my father almost always votes for Republicans. Are these simply matters of opinion on which reasonable people can differ?

- I believe gambling is destructive, while most people in my state think it is a good way to raise public funds. I am uneasy about the implications of cloning research, while many see it as the way to eradicate dread diseases. Are public policy options simply a matter of political preference?

From small matters like the wisdom of the designated hitter rule in baseball to important matters like the morality of the death penalty, there seems to be no one truth that is evident to all. More tellingly, the designated hitter rule and the death penalty are placed on an equal footing. Our culture assumes that they are both simply matters of judgment about which reasonable persons may disagree.

What is truth? Perhaps the question comes down to what is truth for you, truth for me, truth for each person. These personal truths seem to emerge from our differing experiences so that truths are as numerous as the vast array of distinct individual histories. Even when truth escapes the confines of personal life it remains tied to the experience of particular groups. Thus, truth appears to be different for African Americans than for whites, different for women than for men, different for Asians than for Westerners. We are aware that even the once commonly shared American Story is no longer cohesive. European Americans may celebrate Columbus's discovery of the new world while Native Americans grieve it as the first incursion in a savage conquest. White Americans may look reverently at the founding fathers while African Americans see only slaveholders who counted their chattel as three-fifths human. What is truth?

Alasdair MacIntyre notes the absence of shared truth about moral issues in our society: "The most striking feature of contemporary moral utterance is that so much of it is used to express disagreements; and the most striking feature of the debates in which these disagreements are expressed is their interminable character. I do not mean by this just that such debates go on and on and on—although they do—but also that they apparently can find no terminus. There seems to be no rational way of securing moral agreement in our culture."[3] MacIntyre is right about the interminable character of societal disagreements over dramatic issues such as abortion, gun control, and homosexuality. But for the most part, our more ordinary disagreements are quickly "resolved" simply by living comfortably with our differences. We believe that diverse personal perspectives should be respected and so we tolerate a wide range of beliefs, affirming that all persons have a right to their own moral, political, and religious "truths." The principle is so certain that we respect the right of others to believe in alien abductions, the curative power of pyramids, and the global reach of the Trilateral Commission. Although we think some views are silly, even outlandish, we are content to allow people the space for their convictions as long as they do not intrude on the space reserved for our own convictions. We have our truths, others have their truths, and we are all suspicious of anyone who claims to have THE truth.

Segmentation and Privatization

Certain deep characteristics of our culture affect the way we understand truth as well as shape the character of the truths we affirm. One especially noticeable cultural characteristic is the *segmentation* of social structures into distinct subsystems. Our society is no longer dominated by great institutions that establish cultural norms while providing goods and services for the majority of the populace. Instead, the social system is segmented into differentiated subsystems that function to meet the specialized needs of various subgroups within the society. Education, for example, is no longer a unified system with agreed-upon goals, methodologies, and institutions. Dick and Jane have gone the way of McGuffey's Readers. From preschools to graduate schools, education is a collection of discrete philosophies, distinct goals, specialized procedures, and diversified curricula, all presided over by independent institutions. Segments of the education "system" are only loosely interrelated; the parts are more visible than the whole, and each of the parts is designed to meet a specialized need with a specialized service.

The mass media provide a striking illustration of segmentation in contemporary culture. In the 1950s and well into the 1960s, AM radio was the only radio for most Americans. Most stations on the AM dial had the same format—"top 40"—which meant that all teenagers and many adults across the country shared the same music. Now, the FM dial is an array of specialty stations offering different styles of music for diverse tastes while AM has become the haven of talk radio, ranging from news to sports to advice. The "Big Three" television networks are a fading memory as cable and satellite systems deliver 40, 80, 120, 200 channels into our homes. Most of these cable channels are designed to appeal to the specialized interests and tastes of increasingly differentiated viewers. National weekly magazines like *The Saturday Evening Post, Look,* and *Life* have disappeared while niche magazines have multiplied, catering to every interest of every demographic subgroup.

Not too long ago, North America was characterized by a cohesive social structure presided over by basic, integrative institutions. Government, business, labor unions, schools, the media, and other unifying elements provided society with comprehensive patterns of understanding. These institutions were not monolithic, of course, and the cultural cohesion they fostered was not absolute. Even so, "the man in the grey flannel suit" and "the establishment" were easily identifiable cultural markers. While the social structure was not unitary, it did provide broad patterns of recognizable, shared meaning. For many, the church was one of society's basic, integrative elements. The church was a community that encompassed a wide range of communal values, shaping life into a whole and providing cohesion to family, school, job, and leisure. Now, even for its members, the church is but one of society's segmented institutions dealing with the specialized area of "religion."

Social segmentation contributes to the *privatization* of decisions. In a highly segmented society such as ours, patterns of belief, patterns of association, and patterns of action are no longer shaped by customary arrangements. Everything is a matter of individual choice and private decision. People do not assume that there are paths that they must follow or authorities to which they are accountable—whether families, or advisers, or systems, or institutions. Instead, persons assume that *they* are the authority deciding which of multiple possibilities to choose. Great social structures shrink before our eyes: government is not trusted, business is not believed, schools are not authorities, for *each one of us* decides whom to trust and what to believe.

Segmented social structures both serve and encourage private decision. We are not confined to deciding if there is a show we want to watch on ABC, CBS, or NBC. Now we can choose among The Discovery Channel, several ESPN channels, A&E, Black Entertainment Network, multiple movie channels, CNBC and MSNBC, two or three shopping networks, MTV and VH1, PBS, Nickelodeon, and more. Cable TV is only an obvious instance of segmented social structures that reinforce the ubiquity of choice. Each one of us decides about everything, secure in the assumption that our choices are ours alone. Others may make different decisions, and that is their right, for the only absolute is the freedom to choose. Privatization of decision may be most apparent in our "private lives," but it is not limited to leisure choices. The arena of personal preference encompasses every area of life. Our culture declares that we are not constrained by family, community, church, profession, or nation. The right to choose is ours alone.

Our society functions on the model of a sprawling shopping mall. Specialty boutiques are scattered randomly throughout the mall, catering to diverse tastes while offering new possibilities and encouraging impulse purchases. The church is confined to religious shops located in one wing of the mall, competing with one another for a dwindling market share. As people wander through society's shopping mall, they are free to choose whether to enter any of the religious boutiques and what, if anything, they will buy.

None of this is meant to paint a nostalgic portrait of the golden past when America was unified, or to curse the destructive fragmentation of contemporary society. Social cohesion can stultify as well as harmonize, and diversity can enrich as well as segment. I do not even intend to suggest a stark contrast between the present and previous generations. Even the 1950s had its beatniks, and contemporary society's segments are oddly conformist. Yet North American culture changes, and life today is different from life in previous generations. It is of more than passing interest to be conscious of cultural changes and to describe them with a measure of accuracy. Unless we are able to discern our situation, we will be as unaware of the forces that shape our lives as we are of the air we breathe.

The Mall within the Church

What is true of our culture is also true within the church. The contemporary church is no longer a community of shared certainty in commonly acknowledged truths. Unwilling to grant authority to creeds, institutions, or persons, we have become impatient with theology, distrustful of doctrine, and indifferent to institutions. Leaders are tolerated in the church only as long as their leadership is in agreement with our own views or confined to matters that are peripheral to our concerns. The church has never been a unified community of unanimous views, of course. A casual reading of the New Testament letters is sufficient to confirm that the church has been characterized by diversity from the beginning. Yet the New Testament letters assume that unity in the faith is a central aim of Christian community. That assumption does not go unquestioned among us.

We live in a pluralistic world, and so we desire a church that is inclusive of the world's rich diversity. Our celebration of diversity goes beyond appreciation for the natural variety of race, ethnicity, gender, and personal gifts, however. We also make room in the church for a wide variety of preferences, opinions, convictions, and beliefs. Many people within the church simply assume that theological and moral truths are different for different Christians. Since a wide variety of beliefs emerges from a wide range of personal and communal experience, even *Christian* beliefs are thought to be diverse.

Several years ago, a "worship team" gathered at one of the church's national conference centers to plan the Sunday service. Since the theme of one of the week's conferences was the Nicene Creed, it was suggested that the Creed should be confessed following the sermon. The proposal was met with uncomfortable silence until one team member suggested brightly that "we could say the Creed slowly, giving people time to stand for the parts they agree with and sit down for the parts they disagree with."

Standing and sitting to express agreement and disagreement with the Creed may seem particularly silly—or particularly tragic—but it is a parable of the way things are in the church. "God alone is Lord of the conscience,"[4] we say, and so it seems that all beliefs should be respected in the church—even encouraged—and that no attempt should be made to impose one "version" of the truth. The church lives within the culture, and so it is not surprising that the culture's acceptance of multiple truths is found within the church.

There was a time, not too long ago, when the culture's confidence in the demonstrable truths of science extended to certainty about universal social, moral, and religious truths. There was widespread social agreement about such verities as "justice," "democracy," "Christian morality," and "the American way." No longer. Court TV, low voter turnouts, network sitcoms, Iran–Contra, the Clinton impeachment, and the Florida vote count in the 2000 presidential election all demonstrate the lack of social consensus and the assumption that truth is relative to different persons or groups. Before the term *postmodern* became stylish, sociologist Peter Berger described the implications of all this for the church. Noting that the English word *heresy* comes from the Greek word *hairein*, "to choose," Berger describes the contemporary situation: "In the matter of religion . . . the modern individual is faced not just with the opportunity but with the necessity to make choices as to his beliefs. This fact constitutes the heretical imperative in the contemporary situation. Thus heresy, once the occupation of marginal and eccentric types, has become a much more general condition; indeed, heresy has become universalized."[5]

Berger's clever play on the common root for *heresy* and *choice* may highlight the contemporary unimaginability of heresy as well as the universality of choice. What would count as heresy today? Are heresy trials conceivable in the church? A group of New Testament scholars dismisses the authenticity of Jesus' words and deeds, some theologians reject the incarnation, a bishop denies the resurrection, many preachers ignore the cross, and thousands of Christians believe in reincarnation. Yet all of these views are seen as choices, not heresy.

What is truth? Is it nothing more than personal preference or group opinion? Certainly, we are uncomfortable with the idea that a person or an institution could determine what is "true" and compel our assent. But that is only part of the story. We are also uncomfortable with the idea that there are no standards of truth, no bases for shared conviction. The Presbyterian Church's centuries-old Historic Principles affirm that "God alone is Lord of the conscience," but they also declare that "no opinion can be either more pernicious or more absurd than that which brings truth and falsehood upon a level, and represents it as of no consequence what a man's opinions are."[6] We know that both truth and falsehood have consequences. What people believe to be true does matter, and sometimes it is a matter of life and death.

What is truth—that all races are equal in human dignity, or that some races are inferior to other races? What is truth—that diseases are God's punishment for sin, or that diseases are natural occurrences for which cures should be found? What is truth—that a fetus is a human person at conception, or at birth? What is truth—that all peoples have the right of political self-determination, or that states have the right to preserve their national integrity? Clearly, what we believe to be true has consequences for personal, group, and political behavior. The consequences are sufficiently weighty that the search for truth is vital. Without knowledge of the truth, we become captive to the will of a majority or to the force of a minority.

Who Is Truth?

"What is truth?" Pilate asked. We don't know whether he really wanted to know or simply wanted to end an annoying interrogation, whether he was earnest or cynical. However, we do know that the question he asked is vitally important, perhaps even a matter of life and death. But Pilate did not get an answer to his question. The trial scene ends abruptly as the narrative moves on to the horrors of a lynch mob, torture, ridicule, and death. But if we are familiar with the Gospel according to John, we already know the Bible's answer to Pilate's question.

Earlier in John's narrative we read about a baffling conversation that Jesus had with disciples who were confused and frightened by his talk of betrayal, departure, and death (see John 13:21—14:7). On the night of the last supper he would share with his disciples, Jesus announced that he was leaving and that he was giving his disciples a new commandment: to love one another as he had loved them. Ignoring Jesus' announcement of the commandment to love, Peter blurted out the obvious, direct question, "Lord, where are you going?" But he did not get a direct answer, only the vague response that where

Jesus was going Peter could not follow. Peter impetuously pledged to follow Jesus to any destination, only to be told that he would betray his master, not follow him.

Then, to an increasingly mystified group of disciples, Jesus spoke words that are now a familiar part of the Christian funeral liturgy: "Let not your hearts be troubled; believe in God, believe also in me. In my Father's house are many rooms; if it were not so, would I have told you that I go to prepare a place for you? And when I go and prepare a place for you, I will come again and will take you to myself, that where I am you may be also. And you know the way where I am going" (John 14:1–4, RSV).

Thank God for Thomas—"doubting Thomas"—who gives voice to the question exploding in everyone's mind. "Lord, we do not know where you are going; how can we know the way?" Jesus' reply to Thomas's question is the response to Pilate's question as well: "I am the way, and the truth, and the life." Throughout John's Gospel, Jesus is proclaimed as the one who dwelt among us "full of grace and truth," the one who came to "bear witness to the truth," the one who promises "the Spirit of truth," the one who *is* truth! What is truth? John relates the answer before the question is asked: Jesus of Nazareth, Jesus the Christ, is truth!

What is truth? The paramount truth in our world is not a fact, a doctrine, or a private belief. *The Truth* is a person, Jesus Christ, who is God with us and for us. The whole of the New Testament joins John's Gospel in proclaiming that *The Truth*, Jesus Christ, is the truth about God, the truth about us, the truth about the relationship between God and us, and the truth about life among us. The testimony of Scripture is affirmed by two millennia of Christian tradition, from Nicaea to Barmen and beyond. What is truth? Jesus Christ is truth, and that truth is the way, and that way is life!

"The preservation of the truth" is the church's calling to preserve the good news that Jesus Christ is the way, the truth, the life. The church's primary vocation is not to protect a specific body of dogmatic formulations or to impose rigid tests of doctrinal purity. The church is called to preserve faith in the Truth to which Christ bore witness, the Truth that Christ is, and the Spirit of Truth that abides in us. Truth is the shape of our relationship with God through Christ in the power of the Holy Spirit.

Where Is Truth?

Fans of the 1990s television series *The X-Files* are familiar with the program's tag line: "The truth is out there." *X-Files* truth may be a bit farther out than we are accustomed to go, but the phrase reflects the widespread notion that truth is something that exists someplace beyond us. That is why we *search* for truth and, if we are diligent, *discover* truth. Once we have *found* truth, we must *grasp* truth lest it slip away, and *master* truth so that it does escape us. Our customary terminology seems almost antagonistic, as if truth were an adversary to be tracked down, captured, and controlled. Whether truth is strange and elusive or familiar and approachable, however, the external, objective truth remains "out there," apart from us. The most we can expect to do is hold on to it once we have it in hand, and put it to use.

Everyday ways of expressing our relation to the truth seem oddly inappropriate in relation to the Truth, Jesus Christ. The Truth is not "out there" to be discovered, grasped, mastered, and put to use. Actually, the Bible sees us less as seekers after truth than as fugitives from it. The Truth seeks us out, says John's Gospel, coming among us as one of us: "the Word became flesh and lived among us, and we have seen his glory, the glory as of a father's only son, full of grace and truth" (John 1:14). Thus the Truth is not far from us, says Paul, so we need not ask 'Who will ascend into heaven?' (that is, to bring Christ down) or 'Who will descend into the abyss?' (that is, to bring Christ up from the dead). . . . 'The word is near you, on your lips and in your heart' (Rom. 10:6–8).

The Truth is not "out there," distinct from us as an elusive object mocking our efforts at mastery. Rather, the Truth seeks us out and draws us into Truth itself. Remember that Pilate's question was prompted by Jesus' declaration, "Everyone who belongs to the truth listens to my voice." The church's testimony is that all of us within the community of faith belong to the Truth, to Christ, and all of us within the community of faith are to listen to Truth's own testimony. Truth is in relationship to us, not as a stranger but as a friend, not as quarry but as companion, not as something to be controlled but as Master. We are, then, servants of the Truth rather than those who put truth to use, preservers of our relationship to the Truth rather than conservators of facts, theories, doctrines, dogmas, or traditions. To be sure, the Christian Tradition is not unimportant; facts and theories, doctrines and dogmas, are essential means of articulating the truth of the gospel. Even so, the church's tradition is not a free-standing institutional achievement, but is only derivative from the church's living faithfulness to the Truth itself.

The preservation of the truth, the perpetuation of the church's relationship to the Truth, Jesus Christ, is not *primarily* an intellectual exercise. In the first instance, preservation of the truth is lived faithfulness that is proclaimed in community worship, personal prayer, and multiple forms of discipleship. Secondarily, then, preservation of the truth has a vital intellectual component that tests the church's proclamation in worship, prayer, and discipleship. All worship is not worship of "the Father in spirit and truth" (John 4:23). Some prayers give evidence that "the truth is not in us" (1 John 1:8). Not everything that calls itself discipleship is an expression of love "in truth and action" (1 John 3:18). Because the church must always test itself to be sure that it knows the difference between "the spirit of truth and the spirit of error" (1 John 4:6), preservation of the truth requires its best thinking.

The Truth about the Truth

The film *Jesus Christ Superstar* adds a distinctly contemporary twist to Jesus' interrogation by Pilate. The Roman governor follows his question, "What is truth?" with a brief commentary: "We both have truths. Are mine the same as yours?" Presumably not, since Pilate sent Jesus to his death, but *Superstar's* Pilate pushes the question of truth a step further. The Gospels relate Jesus' testimony that he is the truth. Together with the rest of the New Testament, the Gospels concur that Jesus Christ is the truth about God and us. But how do we know that Jesus' truth was any truer than Pilate's? How do we know that the early church's testimony that Jesus Christ is the truth is true? How can we know the truth about the Truth?

The witness of the Bible and the testimony of the church's tradition is questioned from several angles:

- Religious pluralism calls into question the identification of truth with any one religious tradition. The profusion of old and new religions in American society seems to relativize Christian assertions of exclusive truth, making Jesus Christ into *a* truth among other truths.
- Intellectual skepticism dismisses the truth claims of Christian testimony to incarnation and resurrection and any proclamation that "God was in Christ." Confining the "truth" of Jesus to the truth of his exemplary life and teaching reduces him to one wise and admirable example among many.
- Scholarly dissection of the New Testament Gospels has led some to claim that Jesus said little he is supposed to have said, and that

he did little he was supposed to have done. Voting on the veracity of the Gospels has left a Jesus who is indistinguishable from many of his contemporaries.

Are we left with Pilate's question floating in the vacuum of social, intellectual, and scholarly uncertainty? Are we no better off at the end of this little inquiry than we were at the beginning? No. There is much more to be said, of course, but we are no longer stuck on the rhetorical, seemingly unanswerable question, "What is truth?" The question of truth is now focused on the person of Jesus Christ, not on mental abstractions or intellectual constructions. The church's vocation to preserve the truth is a call to remain faithful to the living Christ rather than to protect its own tradition, theology, or testimony. The church may indeed cherish its tradition, teach its theology, and proclaim its testimony, but it is called to do these things out of loyalty to Christ, not out of ecclesiastical aggressiveness or institutional defensiveness. The gospel is the paramount truth on which hang all other truths about God and ourselves; the truth is preserved through the church's enduring faithfulness to Jesus Christ.

The necessity of truth's preservation is far more than a theoretical proposition or a vague possibility. It is a question of lived faithfulness to Christ who is present among us as the Truth. The reality of truth's preservation is far more than the customary activities of ecclesial life. It is a question of critically testing the church's faithfulness. Truth can never be taken for granted and preservation of the truth is never a casual exercise. Perhaps this is best understood in times when the contrast is clear between idolatry and fidelity to the gospel. There have been times when the church's very existence depended on the preservation and courageous assertion of the truth of Jesus Christ.

Evangelical Truths

The early 1930s were perilous times for Christian faith in Germany. Hitler's rise to power was welcomed by many within the church who saw no conflict between Christianity and the ideals of the Nazi movement. As Hitler consolidated his grip on the nation, the Nazis began to assert authority over the church's life, including a notorious law that excluded from church membership all Christians with Jewish ancestry. Many of the church's pastors and members, bishops and theologians, supported the blend of Nazi ideology and Christian faith. These "German Christians" assumed authority for teaching and church administration in support of the state. A minority of pastors and church members resisted, however. An opposition movement organized a Pastors' Emergency League and issued statements of resistance to the state's incursions into the church's life. The call for a free, confessing church culminated in May 1934 as delegates from Lutheran, Reformed, and United churches met in the town of Barmen to speak a unified word to and for the church. "We believe that we have been given a common message to utter in a time of common need and temptation," they declared. "In view of the errors of the 'German Christians' of the present Reich Church government which are devastating the church . . . , we confess the following evangelical truths."[7] The first of these evangelical truths is an unambiguous proclamation of the Truth:

> "I am the way, and the truth, and the life: no one comes to the Father, but by me." (John 14:6.) "Truly, truly, I say to you, he who does not enter the sheepfold by the door but climbs in by another way, that man is a thief and a robber. . . . I am the door; if anyone enters by me, he will be saved." (John 10:1, 9.)
>
> Jesus Christ, as he is attested for us in Holy Scripture, is the one Word of God which we have to hear and which we have to trust and obey in life and in death.
>
> We reject the false doctrine, as though the church could and would have to acknowledge as a source of its proclamation, apart from and besides this one Word of God, still other events and powers, figures and truths, as God's revelation.[8]

In its Theological Declaration, the Confessing Church preserved the truth by proclaiming *The Truth*, Jesus Christ the living Lord. Barmen does not set *a* truth or *its* truth beside other truths in the assumption that reasonable persons might choose any of the available options. Instead, Barmen sets the Truth, Jesus Christ, over against anything that departs from the gospel so that the church can be sustained in loyalty to God.

Barmen's preservation of the truth was a matter of life and death for the church. Perhaps the preservation of the truth is always a matter of life and death for the church, perhaps especially in times when the threat is not obvious or dramatic. Barmen's abiding significance is far more than an inspiring historical instance of ecclesial courage. The Presbyterian Church (U.S.A.) has included the Theological Declaration of

Barmen in its *Book of Confessions* as a clear and present declaration that the church is always called to live in the way of truth that is Jesus Christ.

Yet the truth about the Truth is not always self-evident, and the truth of the gospel is always called into question by cultural, intellectual, and even religious realities. The questions cannot be dismissed, for they are real, and can be posed in the search for truth. In our time, two matters are particularly pressing: doubts about the reliability of the biblical witness, and religious pluralism. If the church is to know and preserve the truth, it must grapple honestly with both.

Notes

1. Iain Pears, *An Instance of the Fingerpost* (New York: Riverhead Books, 1998), p. 615.
2. Frederick Buechner, *Telling the Truth: The Gospel as Tragedy, Comedy, and Fairy Tale* (San Francisco: Harper & Row, 1977), p. 14.
3. Alasdair MacIntyre, *After Virtue*, 2nd ed. (Notre Dame, Ind.: University of Notre Dame Press, 1984), p. 6.
4. *Book of Order*, Presbyterian Church (U.S.A.) (Louisville: Office of the General Assembly, 2002), G-1.0301a. (Hereafter *Book of Order*.)
5. Peter L. Berger, *The Heretical Imperative* (Garden City, N.Y.: Doubleday, Anchor Books, 1979), pp. 30–31.
6. *Book of Order*, G-1.0304.
7. The Theological Declaration of Barmen, in *The Book of Confessions*, Presbyterian Church (U.S.A.) (Louisville: Office of the General Assembly, 2002), 8.08–09. (hereafter *The Book of Confessions* or *BC*.)
8. Ibid., 8.10–12.

The Truth Will Make You Free

Monroe told the story of Christ from divine birth to bloody crucifixion. He included all the famous details and, while keeping it simple, he summoned all the eloquence he could. When he'd finished, he sat back waiting for a reaction.

Esco said, "And you say all this took place some time ago?"

Monroe said, "Two thousand years, if you consider that some time ago."

"Oh, I'd call that a stretch all right," Esco said. He looked at his hands where they hung from the wrists. He flexed the fingers and looked at them critically as if trying the fittings of a new implement. He thought on the story awhile and then said, "And what this fellow come down for was to save us?"

"Yes," Monroe said.

"From our own bad natures and the like?"

"Yes."

"And they still done him like they did? Spiked him up and knifed him and all?"

"Yes indeed," Monroe said.

"But you say the story's been passed around some hundred-score years?" Esco said.

"Nearly."

"So to say, a long time."

"A very long time."

Esco grinned as if he had solved a puzzle and stood up and slapped Monroe on the shoulder and said, "Well, about all we can do is hope it ain't so."

—Charles Frazier, *Cold Mountain* [1]

Do the Gospels give reliable witness to Jesus' birth, life, teachings, death, and resurrection? It would seem that an understanding of Jesus Christ as Truth depends in some measure on the truthfulness of the primary accounts about Jesus Christ. And yet the credibility of the New Testament witness is precisely what is being questioned by persons within the church as well as outside the faith. From Episcopal bishop John Shelby Spong's glib critique of historic Christian faith to the scholarly historicism of "The Jesus Seminar," the New Testament Gospels are assumed to be a mixture of naiveté, error, wishful thinking, and deception, poured over a kernel of historical fact.

Members of the Jesus Seminar use colored marbles to vote on what in the Gospels they believe is "true" and what is not. The tally of red, pink, grey, and black balls announces the Jesus Seminar's opinions, separating what Jesus really said and did from what may be authentic, what probably is not genuine, and what surely is an invention of the church. Bishop Spong seems to be able to make these distinctions on his own. In any case, the result is a severe restriction and broad reinterpretation of biblical testimony. Once "fabrications" have been stripped away, the pared-down evidence does not produce a consistent new picture of Jesus, however. Multiple attempts to discover the authentic Jesus result in multiple depictions of Jesus, ranging from an illegitimate lad who married and fathered children, to a charismatic wonder-worker, an enlightened mystic, a revitalization movement founder, a countercultural Jewish peasant, a homespun Cynic philosopher, and more. We meet these Jesuses "for the first time" in constructions that dismiss the canonical Gospels as reliable sources for our understanding of Jesus. Although the constructions vary, they share two common assumptions: that Jesus' birth was ordinary and that his death was final.

The current search for "the essential Jesus" is nothing new. In the nineteenth century, some biblical interpreters set out to recover "the historical Jesus." Using the insights and techniques of historical scholarship, they attempted to free Jesus from what they understood to be the constraints of church dogma and the burden of popular piety. Their aim was to present an objective life of Jesus that would stand the test of historical scrutiny. But Albert Schweitzer, an acclaimed New Testament scholar before he devoted his life to humanitarian work in Africa, unmasked the illusions of historical scholarship. He showed that attempts to recover "the historical Jesus" were not the exercises in disinterested, objective historical research that their authors imagined them to be. In his 1906 book *The Quest of the Historical Jesus,*

Schweitzer demonstrated that the so-called historical Jesus portrayed in nineteenth-century biographies was really a modern Jesus created in the image of the times. The Jesus of historical scholarship looked suspiciously like the scholars themselves, conforming to contemporary standards of bourgeois respectability and conventional morality. Twentieth-century "lives of Jesus" also appear as oddly modern depictions that reflect their authors' preferences. Like Schweitzer, then, many contemporary biblical scholars and theologians have debunked Bishop Spong, Marcus Borg, and the Jesus Seminar.[2] Perhaps both nineteenth- and twentieth-century "quests of the historical Jesus" confirm T. W. Manson's aphorism, "By their lives of Jesus ye shall know them."[3]

Schweitzer's century-old critique of the reconstructed lives of Jesus built on nineteenth-century historicism has an eerily contemporary ring. Schweitzer writes of his own time that "modern historical theology has more and more adapted itself to the needs of the man in the street. More and more . . . it makes use of attractive headlines as a means of presenting its results in a lively form to the masses. Intoxicated with its own ingenuity in inventing these, it becomes more and more confident in its cause, and has come to believe that the world's salvation depends in no small measure upon the spreading of its own 'assured results.' . . ."[4] With minor editorial changes, Schweitzer's judgment could be applied to the current work of the Jesus Seminar and its allies.

Before we are too hard on quests of the historical Jesus, however, we must admit that the danger of crafting a Jesus in our own image is not confined to past centuries or to academic historians. The danger is clear and ever-present among us all. The Sunday school "gentle Jesus, meek and mild," the suburban "Jesus the caring helper," the Central American "Jesus the revolutionary liberator," and any number of other Jesuses may be nothing more than our own fabrications, forcing the "historical Jesus" into the mold of our preferences and needs. The church's urgent task is always to test its preferred "Jesus" by the accounts of the Gospels and other New Testament writings.

But what assurance do we have that the New Testament Gospels themselves are not merely the projected preferences and needs of first-century Christians? Some critics assert that because the Gospels are interpretations of Jesus by early Christian communities we have no access to the real Jesus of history. All we have, they say, is the proclamation of the early church, and that church proclamation is shaped by the religious needs and institutional dynamics of the early community. Of course it is true that the New Testament Scriptures are the proclamation of the early church, but it does not follow that the church's proclamation is an invention. The early church believed that its proclamation was good news, and that the good news was about something that was true. Because the apostolic witness understood itself to be proclamation of the truth, it makes sense to hear what the earliest Christians have to say, and to hear it on their own terms before imposing our terms on them.

The Good News

The story of Jesus is told in four Gospels: Mark, Luke, Matthew, and John. While these Gospels tell Jesus' story, they are not histories of his life and death. Instead, the Gospels are proclamations of *the* gospel, presentations of the good news of God's salvation for all people through the life, death, and resurrection of one person, Jesus of Nazareth.

Mark's Gospel begins with the ambiguous announcement, "The beginning of the gospel of Jesus Christ, the Son of God" (Mark 1:1, NIV). Is Mark simply introducing the start of his narrative about Jesus? Or is he signaling the commencement of Jesus' ministry of announcing the good news that God's Way has come near? Or is Mark heralding the beginning of his own proclamation of the good news of Jesus Christ? Perhaps he is doing all three things. The gospel is bound to the life and teaching of Jesus of Nazareth, the gospel is inaugurated in Jesus' own proclamation of God's reign, and the gospel is the good news of redemption in Jesus Christ. The whole gospel is proclaimed in the four Gospels and throughout the New Testament.

The Gospels proclaim the gospel as they narrate the story of Jesus. Because their purpose is to tell good news, they do not strive for chronological precision like an encyclopedia entry, or for comprehensive history like a biography. The Gospels proceed with Jesus' story at an uneven pace, relating some things but skipping over a lot, glossing over "big" events while lingering on little ones. Events are not related simply because they happened, but because they reveal God's new Way in the world and show the new way people can live. Because each of the four New Testament Gospels tells the story a bit differently, they present complementary accounts of the significance of Jesus. They are not indifferent to "what really happened," but their main concern is to disclose the meaning of what happened. The Gospels are *interpretations* of the life of Jesus, not merely factual accounts. But the Gospels are interpretations of *the life of Jesus*, not fabrications of the early church. Mark, Luke, Matthew, and John—like the letters and other writings of the New Testament—provide us with narratives that proclaim Jesus Christ and the new life in Christ.

The New Testament writings constitute the earliest Christian expressions of the good news of Jesus Christ and its significance for the world's redemption. Although they are reliable accounts, their interest in the meaning of the gospel reflects more than a concern for accuracy. The New Testament writers understood that we only comprehend the truth of the gospel when we receive the gospel as good news for ourselves. Thus, they did not write simply to provide information; they wrote to engender and to strengthen faith. The evangelists' intention is clear in John's acknowledgment that his Gospel was written "so that you may come to believe that Jesus is the Messiah, the Son of God, and that through believing you may have life in his name" (John 20:31).

Faith Is a Verb

Christian belief is sometimes mistaken for rational assent to certain truths. The Nicene and Apostles' Creeds, for instance, may seem to ask church members to acknowledge a series of facts: God is the creator of heaven and earth, Jesus Christ was raised from the dead, there is a Holy Spirit, the church is God-given, etc. A primary reason for this misunderstanding is the inability of the English language to express a word found in the original Greek of the New Testament. The Greek word for "faith" is *pistis*. It is a particularly rich word that embraces belief, trust, and loyalty. Faith in God is confident belief about God, living trust in God, and steadfast loyalty to God. The verb form of this rich Greek word is *pisteuo*. Our problem is that we have no English verb form of the noun *faith*. We do not say, "I faith, you faith, he/she/it faiths; we faith, you faith, they faith." Instead, we rely on the English verb *believe*. The result is that our language, our thinking, and perhaps even our living are narrowed as trust and loyalty are eclipsed by belief. Faith and faithing are reduced to belief and believing.

Surely faith does entail the mind's assent to certain realities. Faith *believes* that Jesus was born, and that he lived, and that he was crucified, and that he was raised from the dead. Faith also *believes* that "the Word became flesh and lived among us" (John 1:14), and that "in Christ God was reconciling the world to himself" (2 Cor. 5:19), and that "through him God was pleased to reconcile to himself all things, . . . by making peace through the blood of his cross" (Col. 1:20), and that

"Jesus our Lord . . . was raised for our justification (Rom. 4:25). Faith encompasses belief, both in events and in the meaning of events, but it is broader than the rational acceptance of truths. "You believe that God is one;" says James, "you do well. Even the demons believe—and shudder" (James 2:19). Faith also entails a relationship with the God in whom we believe, a bond characterized by trust and loyalty.

To have faith in God is to be open to God's self-revelation, to rely on the truth and integrity of what God has done in Christ. The Presbyterian Church (U.S.A.)'s most recent confessional statement expresses faith's trust:

> In life and in death we belong to God.
>> Through the grace of our Lord Jesus Christ,
>>> the love of God,
>>>> and the communion of the Holy Spirit,
>> we trust in the one triune God, the Holy One of Israel,
>>> whom alone we worship and serve.[5]

"Faithing" God is trusting God to be who God has shown himself to be in Christ, and trusting God to do what he has promised. In Christ we know the God who is reliable, and so we know that God may be trusted, worshiped, and served. Since our trusting worship and service are the shape of a relationship that endures, faith is also characterized by loyalty—active trust extending through time. Just as God remains faithful to us, so we are called to remain loyal to God, trusting God's goodness though all of life's circumstances. The psalmist expresses faith's loyalty:

> Vindicate me, O Lord,
>> for I have walked in my integrity,
>>> and I have trusted in the Lord without wavering.
> Prove me, O Lord, and try me;
>> test my heart and mind.
> For your steadfast love is before my eyes,
>> and I walk in faithfulness to you.
>
>> *(Ps. 26:1)*

Faith *believes* in the truth of God in Christ, faith *trusts* the truth of God in Christ, and faith remains *loyal* to the truth of God in Christ. Yet English translations of the New Testament obscure the breadth and depth of faith by translating *pisteuo* as "believe." Perhaps it would enrich our understanding if, occasionally, we were to substitute a new verb form—*to faith*—when we encounter *believe* in an English translation of the Bible:

> The time is fulfilled, and the kingdom of God has come near; repent, and *faith* the good news. (Mark 1:15)

> I *faith*; help my *unfaithing*! (Mark 9:24)

> For God so loved the world that he gave his only Son, so that everyone who *faiths* him may not perish but may have eternal life. (John 3:16)

> But how are they to call on one in whom they have not *faithed*? And how are they to *faith* one of whom they have never heard? (Rom. 10:14)

It might also enrich our understanding to add the words *trust* and *loyalty* when we encounter *believe*: "But these [things] are written so that you may come to believe that Jesus is the Messiah, the Son of God, *trust in Jesus the Messiah, the Son of God, and remain loyal to the Messiah, the Son of God*, that through *believing, trusting, and remaining loyal* you may have life in his name" (John 20:31; italics added).

None of this is meant to suggest that belief is unimportant or that belief is a peripheral element of faith. Nevertheless, belief in the truth of Jesus Christ must be accompanied by a relationship to the Truth who is Jesus Christ, a relationship of trust and loyalty. We might say that belief is the foundation of faith, for we must know and believe the truth about God in Christ in order to trust God and remain loyal to God's Truth. Concern for the truth of the gospel is clear in Paul's warning to the Galatians that "there are some who are confusing you and want to pervert the gospel of Christ" and in his determination that "the truth of the gospel might be preserved" (Gal. 1:7; 2:5, RSV). This preservation of the truth was not merely an intellectual exercise in doctrinal purity, for Paul understood the integral relationship between right belief and faithful living. "We must no longer be children," Paul wrote, "tossed to and fro and carried about by every wind of doctrine. . . . But speaking the truth in love, we must grow up in every way into him who is the head, into Christ, from whom the whole body, joined and knit together by every ligament with which it is equipped, as each is working properly, promotes the body's growth in building itself up in love" (Eph. 4:14–16, RSV).

Throughout its history, the Christian community's concern for the truth about God and ourselves has been far more than a fascination with intellectual orthodoxy. What we believe about Jesus Christ makes a difference in how we understand God's Way in the world, and how we live our way in the world. What we believe to be true shapes the way we live. The very word *orthodoxy* is formed from two Greek words that mean "right (*orthos*) praise" (*doxa*). Orthodoxy is the proper praise of God in worship and service, the true service of God in all of life. Together with John's Gospel, all New Testament proclamation is written so that we who read and hear might have faith, and that through our faith we might have life. Biblical proclamation is a call, and we must decide whether or not we will respond.

Call and Response

Throughout the Gospels, Jesus' presence elicits responses from people. The narratives of his encounters with strangers and friends and enemies, and the varied reactions from these people, are not merely historical accounts, however. Contemporary readers and hearers are also called to make their own response. "Who do you say that I am?" Jesus asked his disciples (Matt. 16:15). It is also our question.

Although there are obvious differences in emphasis and tone among the Gospels, all four narrate a ministry of Jesus that is grounded in the faith of Israel and marked by teaching and healing—a ministry that proclaims the good news of God's reign and offers wholeness to humankind. A new thing happens in Jesus' words and deeds, but it is never compellingly obvious, as if all who hear what he says and see what he does are moved to acknowledge the presence of God's new Way in the world. Yet the presence of Jesus calls for decision; his words and deeds demand a response. What is true within the Gospel narratives remains true, for we too respond, and we too decide. Is this Jesus the Truth? Has the Way of God drawn near in him? If so, what is the shape of God's reign? Will we choose to live within it?

The Gospels agree on the distinctive features of Jesus' ministry: he proclaimed the reign of God, he healed, he taught, he associated with outsiders, and he was executed. Yet the meaning of Jesus' proclamation, his healing and teaching, his friendships and enmities, his life and death, is not self-evident. How do we understand it, and how shall we respond to it?

The healing narratives in the Gospels cry out for response. A decision must be made—not about the possibility of the miraculous, but about the one who performs the miracles. The necessity for response is apparent in the healing of a "demoniac . . . blind and mute" (see Matt. 12:22–28). A demon-possessed man who could neither see nor speak was brought to Jesus. With a dramatic economy of words, Matthew states simply, "and he cured him." What was the response to this wonder-filled healing? Some people responded with a question: "Can this be the Son of David?" Notice that their response was not a declaration of faith—"This is the Son of David"—but a question. Others had a quite different reaction, however, and theirs *was* a declaration: "It is only by Beelzebul, the ruler of the demons, that this fellow casts out the demons." Here, as throughout the Gospels, it is impossible not to respond. Do Jesus' actions open up God's Way in the world? Or do they present a mistaken picture of God's reign? Or worse, a deceitful picture? Matthew's Gospel relates the negative response clearly, while only hinting at a positive response. The narrative leaves the way open for our own response.

Jesus' words also present occasions for decision. Parables are a characteristic form of Jesus' teaching, presenting the possibilities of God's new Way in the world. Jesus told stories about everyday realities involving laborers, bosses, merchants, neighbors, rulers, and other familiar figures. Yet into the midst of everydayness a jarring element intrudes, compelling our attention. What shepherd in his right mind would abandon the whole flock to look for one lost sheep? What faithful Jewish woman would put yeast in Passover bread? What sensible farmer would throw his seed on paths and rocks? These stories display something about God's Way in the world, but what is it? And what are we supposed to do? Little wonder that even those with ears to hear did not always know what to make of Jesus' teaching.

Another characteristic of Jesus' ministry was his practice of eating and drinking with all sorts of people, from the anonymous thousands, to tax collectors, to just plain "sinners." What was the response to Jesus' indiscriminate eating and drinking? Some accused him of drunkenness and gluttony. Many hated him for violating the boundaries of faithful covenantal observance. Others, like Zacchaeus, found repentance and new life in Jesus' open hospitality.

The Gospels proceed from accounts of Jesus' words and deeds to extended narratives of his suffering and death. In agonizing detail they present Jesus' death, not as the tragic end of a teacher and healer, but as the consequence and climax of his teaching and healing. The overriding response to Jesus was to kill him! Even Jesus' resurrection—God's startling vindication of Jesus' ministry—did not evoke a uniform response. The Gospels narrate the resurrection story differently, from Mark's disturbingly open-ended account to the more fully developed versions of Matthew, Luke, and John. Yet all the Gospels agree on this central point: the crucified Jesus has been raised from death to new life. Responses to this reality range from fear, doubt, disbelief, and ridicule, to amazement, understanding, joy, love, and worship. As with Jesus' words and deeds, his crucifixion and resurrection demand a response and require a decision. Is this the Truth?

The Gospels are not "lives of Jesus." But we could say that they are "deaths of Jesus," for his crucifixion provides the defining angle of vision on his life. Was Jesus a caring healer who moved with compassion among the sick and disabled? Yes, but if that was all he was, why was he executed for it? Was Jesus a wise teacher whose sayings pointed the way to a fulfilling life? Again, yes, but if he was only that, why were people so outraged that they crucified him? Was Jesus a good man who served the needs of the poor and oppressed? Of course, but if that is all there is, why was he killed?

It is all too easy for us to see Jesus as an admirable fellow who was misunderstood by his opponents while we, on the other hand, understand his goodness. The Gospels tell a different story. Jesus' opponents understood him well. They knew that the Way of God proclaimed by Jesus turned "the way things are" upside down, requiring a radical reorientation of life. Jesus is not a confirmation of human aspirations, but the one whose words and deeds proclaim something radically new, often in the face of human aspirations.

What are we to make of the Jesus we encounter in the Gospels? We are not given an "objective" Jesus, but a challenge to customary ideas about God, people, the world, and the shape of faithful living. Neither are we given "a riddle wrapped in a mystery inside an enigma,"[6] but a clear testimony to the presence of Emmanuel, God with us. Matthew, Mark, Luke, and John proclaim the significance of Jesus Christ, inviting us to answer who *we* say that he is, beckoning us to trust that Jesus is the Truth, the good news about God and God's Way among us.

Call and *Response*

Jesus Christ: the two words are so bound together that we understand why children may think Christ is Jesus' last name. *Christ* is not a name, of course; it is a confession of faith. "Who do you say that I am?" Jesus asked Peter. Peter replied, "You are the Messiah [the Christ]" (Mark 8:29). *Christos* (Christ), the Greek word for the Hebrew *meshiach* (Messiah), is the central affirmation of the earliest Christian community: Jesus is the Christ.

On the surface, it may appear that the Gospels tell the story of *Jesus* while the rest of the New Testament proclaims *Christ.* Characteristically, the four Gospels speak of "Jesus" while the rest of the New Testament refers to "Jesus Christ," or just "Christ." Moreover, the Gospels narrate the life and teachings of Jesus while the rest of the New Testament virtually ignores Jesus' words and deeds, focusing exclusively on the significance of crucifixion and resurrection. Paul goes so far as to say, "Even though we once knew Christ from a human point of view, we know him no longer in that way" (2 Cor. 5:16).

This obvious difference in perspective has led some to oppose the "simple message" of Jesus found in the Gospels to the early church's "elaborated theology" of Christ. This contrast does not accurately represent either the Gospels or the New Testament letters, however. (It is worth remembering that the Gospels were written *after* Paul's letters.) Both Gospels and letters disclose the significance of Jesus Christ. Although different types of biblical writing approach the reality of Jesus Christ in distinctive ways, the whole New Testament is unified in its affirmation that the human Jesus and the risen Christ are one. Jesus of Nazareth cannot be understood apart from the risen Christ; the risen Christ is incomprehensible apart from the human Jesus.

And yet it is not uncommon for Jesus Christ to be split apart. Some see Jesus as a revered teacher who said many wise things about God and life, but not as the risen, living Christ. Others see the risen Christ as the present power of God, yet disconnected from the Jesus of Nazareth who lived and died in Palestine. Divorcing Jesus and Christ is an old temptation. Within the New Testament itself there is evidence of the struggle to maintain the essential continuity between the Jesus of history and the risen Christ who is present within the community of faith.

In Hebrews we find an explicit attempt to counter overemphasis on the Jesus of history by asserting Jesus' superiority over angels, Moses, and all priests. Jesus Christ is more than messenger, prophet, or priest; Jesus Christ is "the reflection of God's glory and the exact imprint of God's very being" (Heb. 1:3).

In the letters of John we see an explicit attempt to counter overemphasis on the risen Christ by asserting the reality of the incarnation. "Many deceivers have gone out into the world," writes John, "those who do not confess that Jesus Christ has come in the flesh" (2 John 7). John is firm in stating that we can know the truth only by recognizing that "every spirit that confesses that Jesus Christ has come in the flesh is from God, and every spirit that does not confess Jesus is not from God" (1 John 4:2–3). The struggle within the New Testament to maintain the unity of the human Jesus and the risen Christ testifies to the centrality of that unity for Christian faith and life.

Two of the earliest Christian heresies—mistaken understandings of the gospel—are Ebionism and Docetism. The Ebionites claimed that Jesus was simply a human being, a prophet like Moses, Elijah, and others. Docetists claimed that Jesus was a divine being who only appeared to be human. Confronted by these one-sided views of Jesus Christ, the church had to clarify faith so that there would be no misunderstanding of the inseparable reality, *Jesus Christ.*

One-sided views are not confined to early church history. Within the contemporary church there are ample instances of exclusive focus on the Jesus of history or the risen Christ. Some within the church look to the "Jesus of the Gospels" as an example of inclusive love who provides a model for human compassion and justice. The significance of crucifixion–resurrection is slighted, ignored, or even denied. Yet disregarding the cosmic reality of the living Christ reduces Jesus to a figure from the distant past whose relevance to contemporary life is remote. Why, if Jesus is not the risen, living Christ of God, should he be our moral exemplar rather than Confucius, Gandhi, or George Washington? Even if we prefer the moral leadership of Jesus to that of others, what power does a long-ago and faraway Jesus have to transform our lives?

Others in the church look to "the living Christ" as a powerful presence who can provide resources for the achievement of abundant life. Jesus' human life is seen only as a miracle-filled prelude to his saving death and resurrection, or even as an embarrassment. Maintaining the unity of *Jesus Christ* is a continuing task of the Christian community if it is to proclaim faithfully the good news of God's Way rather than the tired tale of our own ways.

Jesus Christ, the Icon of God

Two walls of my office are covered with reproductions of Russian and Greek icons. These paintings of biblical scenes, Jesus Christ, and saints of the church are central to the faith and life of Eastern Orthodox Christians. In Orthodox piety, icons are more than illustrations; they represent the truth of what they depict. The Greek word *eikon*, often translated "image," means a visible manifestation of reality. It is in this sense that the letter to the Colossians proclaims boldly that Jesus Christ is "the image [*eikon*] of the invisible God. . . . For in him all the fullness of God was pleased to dwell" (Col. 1:15, 19).

God is a mystery, we sometimes say, an unknowable reality beyond all human attempts at comprehension. The "otherness" of God is not a modern discovery, however. Isaiah spoke the word of the Lord centuries ago:

> For my thoughts are not your thoughts,
>> nor are your ways my ways, says the LORD.
> For as the heavens are higher than the earth,
>> so are my ways higher than your ways
>> and my thoughts than your thoughts.
>
>> (Isa. 55:8–9)

The good news is that God does not remain above us, cloaked in dark mystery beyond our comprehension. The gospel of Jesus Christ is the proclamation of God's nearness. Paul illuminates this gospel when he declares, "It is the God who said, 'Let light shine out of darkness,' who has shone in our hearts to give the light of the knowledge of the glory of God in the face of Jesus Christ" (2 Cor. 4:6). Jesus Christ is the icon of God, the one who is the Truth of God.

What do we see when we look into the face of Jesus Christ? We see the loving God who became one with us in a life, in a death, and in a new life. God's Way is made known in the icon of God, Jesus Christ. The image of God in our midst is the crucified and risen Christ, for in his death and new life we see the significance of cross and resurrection for our own lives.

Paul wrote to the company of believers in Corinth, reminding them of the gospel's call, their response, and the continuing call to maintain the Truth: "Now I would remind you, brothers and sisters, of the good news that I proclaimed to you, which you in turn received, in which also you stand, through which also you are being saved, if you hold firmly to the message that I proclaimed to you" (1 Cor. 15:1–2). Similarly, John's first letter begins, "We declare to you what was from the beginning, what we have heard, what we have seen with our eyes, what we have looked at and touched with our hands, concerning the word of life—this life was revealed, and we have seen it and testify to it, and declare to you the eternal life that was with the Father and was revealed to us—we declare to you what we have seen and heard so that you also may have fellowship with us; and truly our fellowship is with the Father and with his Son Jesus Christ. We are writing these things so that our joy may be complete" (1 John 1:1–4).

Paul and John and the entire biblical witness invite us to faith, to a life of believing, trusting, and abiding in the grace of the Lord Jesus Christ, the love of God, and the communion of the Holy Spirit. Throughout the pages of Scripture we encounter narratives and hymns, letters and prophecies, visions and wisdom—all proclaiming the Truth that is "God with us." This Truth is neither the reconstruction of historians nor the projection of the pious nor the dogma of the church. The Truth calls for our response.

Communion

The New Revised Standard Version (NRSV) of the Bible translates a single Greek word, *koinonia,* as "communion," fellowship," "participation," "partnership," "sharing," "contribution," and "taking part." The Greek word is rich and subtle, which is why so many English terms are needed by translators. But the average reader of an English-language Bible has no idea of the relationships that are suggested by the common use of *koinonia.* As it is used in the New Testament, *koinonia* suggests a deep, intimate, abiding relationship that cannot be expressed by weak English words such as "fellowship" or "sharing." The English equivalent that best seems to capture the depth of *koinonia* is "communion." If we were to translate all the New Testament occurrences of *koinonia* by "communion," we might begin to sense the depth and breadth of associations suggested by the term, and the relationship between communion and truth.

Koinonia is used as a means of expressing the deep communion of believers with the triune God, a communion that reflects the very being of the one God—Father Son and Holy Spirit. This communion of believers with God takes shape in a communion among believers that bears the marks of communion with Father Son and Holy Spirit.

> We declare to you what we have seen and heard so that you also may have *communion* with us; and truly our *communion* is with the Father and with his Son Jesus Christ. (1 John 1:3)

I thank my God every time I remember you . . . because of your *communion* in the gospel from the first day until now. (Phil. 1:3, 5)

If then there is any encouragement in Christ, any consolation from love, any *communion* in the Spirit, any compassion and sympathy, make my joy complete: be of the same mind, having the same love, being in full accord and of one mind. (Phil. 2:1, 2)

They devoted themselves to the apostles' teaching and *communion*, to the breaking of bread and the prayers. (Acts 2:42)

Communion within the community is more than a vague expression of togetherness, for it entails shared fidelity to the truth and to truthful living.

If we say we that we have *communion* with [God] while we are walking in darkness, we lie and do not do what is true; but if we walk in the light as he himself is in the light, we have *communion* with one another, and the blood of Jesus his Son cleanses us from all sin. (1 John 1:6–7)

For what partnership is there between righteousness and lawlessness? Or what *communion* is there between light and darkness? (2 Cor. 6:14)

I always thank my God because I hear of your love for all the saints and your faith toward the Lord Jesus. I pray that the *communion* of your faith may become effective when you perceive all the good that we may do for Christ. (Philem. 6)

The New Testament proclaims the truth that Jesus Christ is the Truth. Truth calls for response. The call of Truth and response to Truth are the Way of communion with Truth, and human communion with Truth is Life. Jesus Christ is the Way, the Truth, the Life.

The first General Assembly of the Presbyterian Church in the United States of America, meeting in 1789, adopted a series of "Historic Principles of Church Order." The fourth of these Historic Principles sets forth the way of truth and life:

That truth is in order to goodness; and the great touchstone of truth, its tendency to promote holiness, according to our Savior's rule, "By their fruits ye shall know them." And that no opinion can be either more pernicious or more absurd than that which brings truth and falsehood upon a level, and represents it as of no consequence what a man's opinions are. On the contrary, we are persuaded that there is an inseparable connection between faith and practice, truth and duty. Otherwise, it would be of no consequence either to discover truth or to embrace it.[7]

Scripture proclaims that Jesus Christ is Truth. Scripture also proclaims that response to the Truth is not mere assent, but committed response. Call and response constitute a new Way of communion with the Truth, communion that transforms Life.

Notes

1. Charles Frazier, *Cold Mountain* (New York: Vintage Books, 1997), p. 58.
2. For a clear, accessible treatment see Emory University professor Luke Timothy Johnson's *The Real Jesus* (New York: HarperCollins, 1996).
3. Quoted in Luke Timothy Johnson, *Living Jesus: Learning the Heart of the Gospel* (New York: HarperSanFrancisco, 1999), p. 8.
4. Albert Schweitzer, *The Quest of the Historical Jesus* (New York: Macmillan, 1964), p. 311.
5. A Brief Statement of Faith, *The Book of Confessions*, 10.1.
6. Winston Churchill's description of the Soviet Union in a radio broadcast, October 1, 1939. *The Oxford Dictionary of Quotations*, 3rd ed. (Oxford: Oxford University Press, 1979), p. 149.
7. *Book of Order*, G-1.0304.

We All Believe in One True God?

> Once a friend, a member of my small-town church, astonished me by confiding after worship that she no longer believed in the Trinity . . . "I want one God," she said, adding, "I know the Trinity is supposed to be one God, three in one. But I just can't believe it anymore."
>
> The first thing that popped into my mind was something I couldn't say out loud. It's the *only* phrase I recall from a lengthy Russian Orthodox meditation on the Trinity, that "outside the Trinity, there is only hell."
>
> —Kathleen Norris, *Amazing Grace: A Vocabulary of Grace*[1]

Scripture proclaims Jesus Christ as the Truth, and calls for committed response to the Truth. Proclamation *of* the Truth is also proclamation *about* the Truth, focusing on the crucifixion and resurrection of Jesus. The preaching of the early church proclaimed "Jesus Christ of Nazareth" as the one "whom God raised from the dead" (Acts 3:15; 4:10; 5:30; 10:40; 13:30; 26:8, and throughout the letters of Paul). This unwavering message identified not only "Jesus Christ," but also "God." Who is God? God is the One who raised Jesus from the dead, and the One who raised Jesus from the dead is the same One who raised Israel from slavery. God is not a remote being above or behind the life, death, and resurrection of Jesus, but the One who is intimately and actively involved in the life, death, and resurrection of Jesus. God's involvement is so active, so intimate, that who God is becomes fully known in and through Jesus Christ. In this recognition lies the genesis of what has come to be known as the doctrine of the Trinity. Proclamation of the Good News of Christ's life, death, and resurrection leads to the Trinity. But to many church members, the doctrine of the Trinity may not seem like good news.

My favorite hymn never appears in lists of best-loved hymns, but its tune and text combine to nourish my faith. "Holy God, We Praise Your Name" is an eighteenth-century hymn that recalls Revelation's word portrait of heavenly worship. The final verse of this glorious Te Deum sings forth the one triune God whom alone we worship and adore:

> Holy Father, Holy Son,
> Holy Spirit: Three we name You,
> While in essence only One;
> Undivided God we claim You,
> And adoring bend the knee
> While we own the mystery.[2]

Most Christians agree that the Trinity is a mystery, but many are unwilling to "own" it. Some complain that the arcane relationship between three and one is an unnecessary mathematical puzzle, while others object that Father-Son-Spirit language appears to be inappropriately male. On one level, then, arithmetic calculations can lead to dismissal of Trinity as an irrelevant obscurity. On another level, gender issues can lead to rejection of Trinity as a patriarchal anachronism. It may be with unintended irony that worshipers sing, "We all believe in one true God, Father, Son, and Holy Ghost."[3] Do we *all* believe in one *true* God? Is this one true God identifiable as Father Son and Holy Spirit? Or is God a mystery so complex that each of us is free to imagine God in more familiar and affirming ways?

Mathematical Improbabilities

If the Trinity is nothing more than a mathematical conundrum, church members can hardly be blamed for throwing their hands up in despair. How can one be three and three be one? Even if a theological Einstein were to propose an explanation of one-threeness and three-oneness, it would remain beyond the grasp of ordinary people, irrelevant to faith and to faithful living. Yet Trinity is supposed to be a central element of Christian belief, not a peripheral proposition that can easily be ignored. Perhaps that is why artful explanations are put forward in an attempt to make it all understandable. The illustrations that are offered to help us comprehend Trinity are often curiously "scientific," however. Trinity is like H_2O, we are told, one substance that can appear in three forms—water, ice, and steam. Or, Trinity is like three interlocking circles that overlap in the center and share certain segments while retaining distinct areas. But even if God could be captured by a clever analogy or a simple symbol (an unlikely possibility) what would we have gained? What conceivable difference would it make to our worship or our discipleship? Our prayers are not deepened by addressing them to a sacred chemical compound, and our service is not enlivened by a divine logo. Even if we were to imagine that formulas or graphics are accurate explanations of Trinity, the doctrine would remain an abstraction, without genuine meaning to Christian faith and life.

Little wonder that many Presbyterians agree with Kathleen Norris's friend who can no longer believe in the Trinity. They want one God, not implausible talk about a three-in-one-God and paradoxical talk about one-God-in-three-persons. Trinity confronts many church members with an unnecessary puzzle, prompting one wit to joke that the only thing more difficult to explain than the Trinity is baseball's balk rule! The "problem" of the Trinity is not confined to church members, however. Many ministers preach about a generic "God," and many theologians shy away from Trinitarian language. This leads Karl Rahner to lament: "[D]espite their orthodox confession of the Trinity, Christians are, in their practical life, almost mere 'monotheists.' We must be willing to admit that, should the doctrine of the Trinity have to be dropped as false, the major part of religious literature could well remain virtually unchanged."[4]

And yet we cannot easily dismiss countless other Christians who hold the one triune God so central to faith and life that "outside the Trinity there is only hell." The two oldest creeds in the Presbyterian Church's *Book of Confessions* (the Nicene Creed and the Apostles' Creed) and the two newest (The Confession of 1967 and A Brief Statement of Faith) share an indispensable Trinitarian structure. Baptism in the name of the Father and of the Son and of the Holy Spirit is the reality that binds all Christians together. All of this leads Catherine LaCugna to declare: "The doctrine of the Trinity, which is the specifically Christian way of speaking about God, summarizes what it means to participate in the life of God through Jesus Christ in the Spirit."[5]

On the one hand, then, the Trinity seems to be a theological Rubik's Cube, while on the other hand it is affirmed as the center of Christian faith and life. Where do we begin to make Christian sense of it all?

We Worship and Adore

We begin with congregations at worship. Week in and week out, the church's worship abounds with Trinitarian reference. The Trinity is not peripheral to worship; the Trinity is present at the center of the assembly's praise and prayer. The hymns we sing glorify the one triune God, sometimes in explicit, traditional language and sometimes less directly:

> Holy, holy, holy! Lord God Almighty!
> Early in the morning our song shall rise to Thee;
> Holy, holy, holy! merciful and mighty!
> God in three Persons, blessed Trinity.[6]

> God is here! As we your people
> Meet to offer praise and prayer,
> May we find in fuller measure
> What it is in Christ we share.
> Here, as in the world around us,
> All our varied skills and arts
> Wait the coming of the Spirit
> Into open minds and hearts.[7]

The prayers of the faithful embody the same Trinitarian address to God, while acclamations of praise glorify and thank Father Son and Holy Spirit:

> Almighty God,
> to whom all hearts are open,
> all desires known,
> and from whom no secrets are hid:
> Cleanse the thoughts of our hearts
> by the inspiration of your Holy Spirit,
> that we may perfectly love you
> and worthily magnify your holy name;
> through Jesus Christ our Lord. Amen.[8]

Praise God from whom all blessings flow;

Praise God, all creatures here below;

Praise God above, ye heavenly host;

Praise Father, Son, and Holy Ghost. Amen.[9]

Glory be to the Father,

and to the Son,

and to the Holy Ghost;

As it was in the beginning, is now, and ever shall be,

world without end. Amen, Amen.

Trinitarian language intensifies as the sacraments are celebrated. Baptism in the name of the Father and of the Son and of the Holy Spirit seals our incorporation into the body of Christ, the people of God, and the community of the Holy Spirit. Baptism establishes our communion with Christians of every time and place who share life in the triune God. The great prayer of thanksgiving over the water is structured by the saving acts of God's creative, redemptive, and sanctifying love. Like baptism, Eucharist is deeply grounded in Trinitarian memory, hope, and shared life. All of the Great Prayers of Thanksgiving in the *Book of Common Worship* follow the Trinitarian pattern of thankful praise to God, grateful recalling of the acts of salvation in Jesus Christ, and confident invocation of the Holy Spirit. As we share bread and wine we live the mystery of faith: Christ has died; Christ is risen; Christ will come again! Worship concludes with a benedictory blessing in the grace of the Lord Jesus Christ, the love of God, and the communion of the Holy Spirit:

May God the Father, who raised Jesus Christ from
    the dead,
continually show us loving kindness.
Amen.
May God the Son, victor over sin and death,
grant us a share in the joy of his resurrection.
Amen.
May God the Spirit, giver of light and peace,
renew our hearts in love.
Amen.

May almighty God, the Father, the Son, and the Holy Spirit, continue to bless us.

Amen. Alleluia![10]

The shape and the language of worship are not random and purposeless. Neither are they continuously malleable so that they conform to personal preference or cultural disposition. As worship gives communal voice to Christian faith, the language of liturgy articulates the church's "primary theology." The words of worship—spoken, sung, prayed, and enacted—are the church's foundational expression of faith and faithfulness. Worship's pattern, symbols, and words are not our inventions, but gifts from the communion of saints whose worship voiced praise to God through Christ in the Holy Spirit long before our lips were opened. Throughout Christian history, the liturgy has preserved the Trinitarian heart of Christian faith, even when formal theology neglected it. The pulse of Christian worship regularly rehearses the grace of the Lord Jesus Christ, the love of God, and the communion of the Holy Spirit in the events of salvation.

In worship we speak *of* God by speaking *to* God. The church's primary theology is faithful language addressed to God by the worshiping assembly itself. What we usually think of as theology is really "secondary theology," the church's reflection on the primary theology of its worship in an attempt to give systematic coherence to our thanks and praise. Doxology (primary theology) precedes all faithful (secondary) theology. Faith's grounding in doxology is so fundamental that one contemporary theologian can even ask, "To what extent is it necessary to speak *of* God after having accepted the fact that we speak *from* him and *to* him?"[11]

In our place and time, it *is* necessary to speak *of* God. Doxology necessitates theology because cultural and ecclesial realities now combine to call liturgical language into question. We are no longer sure of the heritage bequeathed to us by our forebears in the faith. The need for "inclusive language" leads some to abandon classical Trinitarian identifications of God. The need for "seeker-friendly" worship leads some to abandon reference to the saving works of Christ in crucifixion and resurrection. Non-Pentecostal worship tends to avoid all but the most formal invocations of the Holy Spirit. The result is what Charles Wiley calls "functional unitarianism." The unitary word *God* is repeated endlessly in worship, eliminating all Trinitarian references, submerging references to the saving acts of the triune God under generalized "love," and serving as an impersonal substitute for personal pronouns. The intention may be understandable, but the result is a strangely abstract deity whose generic dealings with us are more like those on the television shows "Touched by an Angel" and "Joan of Arcadia" than the rich narratives of Scripture.

God with Us

In the Bible, God is not known in clever analogies or mathematical formulas, but through narratives. The Scriptures tell the story of God with people through the stories of Israel and Jesus. As the story is told it becomes clear that God is not a simple deity whose being and whose dealings with people can be captured in an easy definition. Through scriptural accounts we come to know God as loving Creator of all that is, righteous Judge and gracious Reconciler of a hostile world, and creative Builder of free human community. As the biblical story relates God's creating, guiding, judging, reconciling, and sustaining work, it becomes clear that while these actions are distinct, they are not separate. God's creating, redeeming, and sustaining are united in the reality of salvation. Scripture does not narrate God's work as sequential, as if God first created, then redeemed, then forged and nurtured a faithful community. Nor does God alternate among three disconnected works, sometimes creating, sometimes reconciling, sometimes sustaining. The one God is eternally creating, judging, redeeming, reconciling, nurturing, preserving. As God moves among us, we know this One in distinct, yet ever-actual and interrelated ways.

It is often said that the Bible does not contain the doctrine of the Trinity. The statement is true as far as it goes, for the Bible does not contain the *doctrine* of anything. The Bible has no doctrine of creation or atonement, justification or sanctification, inspiration or eschatology. Instead, the Scriptures narrate the presence of God through history, poetry, letters, prophecy, and other writings. Doctrines are our attempts to provide systematic accounts of the various narratives of God with us. The Bible does not contain the *doctrine* of the Trinity, but it does contain a range of accounts that reveal the truth about God. And this truth about God is best expressed as Trinity—as one God the Father, God the Son, and God the Holy Spirit.

As the Scriptures narrate God with us, we do not encounter a self-contained lone being. Instead, we encounter a God whose being is characterized by relationships of love. In love God created a reality other than himself, yet in relationship to himself. In love, the incarnate One restored broken relationships in the life, death, and resurrection of Jesus Christ. In love, the Lord nurtures and sustains new community in the Holy Spirit. Scripture declares that "God is love" (1 John 4:16).

God not only *loves*, creating and recreating relationships of love with and in the world, but God *is* love. The very being of God is love. God acts lovingly because God's very self consists in loving relationship. The God who is love does not express love in general, love as a vague feeling of acceptance and intimacy. Rather, the love of the God who *is* love is expressed in specific acts of love.

When we center our attention on creation we focus on the loving work of God. Yet the biblical witness is clear that creation is not the work of the Father apart from the Son and the Spirit. Creation is the work of the triune God, the action of God the Father through the Son and in the Spirit. When we center our attention on salvation we focus on the loving work of Christ. Yet the biblical witness is clear that salvation is not the work of the Son apart from the Father and the Spirit. Salvation is the work of the triune God, the action of the Father who sends the Son in the power of the Holy Spirit. When we center our attention on the redeemed community we focus on the loving work of the Holy Spirit. Yet the biblical witness is clear that the faith, hope, and love of the church are not the work of the Holy Spirit apart from the Son and the Father. Community and consummation are the work of the triune God, in the Spirit through the Son to the Father.

Throughout the narratives of God's love, Scripture is "unselfconscious" about the divinity of the Son and the Spirit. Apparently, the biblical witnesses felt no need to argue a case, no need to explain how the reality of the one God is thoroughly consistent with differentiated action, and no need to develop a doctrine of the Trinity. Instead, the Scriptures simply state the taken-for-granted presence of the one God in the grace of the Lord Jesus Christ, the love of God, and the communion of the Holy Spirit:

> Indeed, even though there may be so-called gods in heaven or on earth—as in fact there are many gods and many lords—yet for us there is one God, the Father, from whom are all things and for whom we exist, and one Lord, Jesus Christ, through whom are all things and through whom we exist. (1 Cor. 8:5–6)

> In the beginning was the Word, and the Word was with God, and the Word was God. He was in the beginning with God. All things came into being through him, and without him not one thing came into being. (John 1:1–3)

So [Christ] came and proclaimed peace to you who were far off and peace to those who were near; for through him both of us have access in one Spirit to the Father. (Eph. 2:17–18)

And when Jesus had been baptized, just as he came up from the water, suddenly the heavens were opened to him and he saw the Spirit of God descending like a dove and alighting on him. And a voice from heaven said, "This is my Son, the Beloved, with whom I am well pleased. (Matt. 3:16–17)

"I have said these things to you while I am still with you. But the Advocate, the Holy Spirit, whom the Father will send in my name, will teach you everything, and remind you of all that I have said to you." (John 14:26)

There is one body and one Spirit, just as you were called to the one hope of your calling, one Lord, one faith, one baptism, one God and Father of all, who is above all and through all and in all. (Eph. 4:4–6)

These few scriptural sentences are not meant as proofs, or even as a brief catalog of Trinitarian references. They simply illustrate the natural way Scripture assumes the integrity of the triune God whose actions in the world are a differentiated whole. The New Testament does not spell out a developed Trinitarian Christology, but the Scriptures are clear that Jesus was more than a human teacher and prophet: "In Christ God was reconciling the world to himself" (2 Cor. 5:19); "For in him all the fullness of God was pleased to dwell, and through him God was pleased to reconcile to himself all things, whether on earth or in heaven, by making peace through the blood of his cross" (Col. 1:19–20). The New Testament does not elaborate a Trinitarian doctrine of the Holy Spirit, but the Scriptures are clear that the Holy Spirit is more than human spirituality writ large: "the spirit of glory, which is the Spirit of God, is resting on you" (1 Peter 4:14); "Now the Lord is the Spirit, and where the Spirit of the Lord is, there is freedom" (2 Cor. 3:17). The New Testament does not elaborate a Trinitarian theology, but the Scriptures are clear that God is the Father of the Son, the Son of the Father, the Spirit of God and the Spirit of Christ, in relationships of love that flow into the world: "When the Advocate comes, whom I will send to you from the Father, the Spirit of truth who comes from the Father, he will testify on my behalf" (John 15:26).

The Scriptures are unselfconscious, but they do not stand alone. The Bible is accompanied by worshipers and learners, preachers and hearers, readers and interpreters. Because of this diversity—and even through it—the church must always seek to clarify a common understanding of the biblical witness. Shared clarity is not a certain outcome, however, for while inevitable differences of interpretation can be mutually enriching, they can also be divisive and even destructive. Sometimes interpretations are so divergent that the church must make a fundamental decision between starkly opposing versions of the faith, between orthodoxy and heresy, between right worship and wrong choice.

Over the course of its first three centuries the church struggled—sometimes contentiously—to give clear answer to the basic question, "Who is God?" The answer, forged in fidelity to the Scriptural witness, is the doctrine of the Trinity. This doctrine is not an unsuitable teaching about the abstract nature of God, or a barren teaching about God in isolation, or an esoteric presumption to know God's "inner" life. The Trinity is the church's shared clarification of God's self-disclosure, God's freely communicated self-revelation in the person of Christ and the activity of the Spirit.

For Us and Our Salvation

The doctrine of the Trinity was formalized at the ecumenical councils of Nicaea (A.D. 325) and Constantinople (A.D. 381). Although the Nicene Creed was occasioned by sharply divergent interpretations of the scriptural witness, and thus the need for doctrinal clarity, its genesis lay in congregations. In local Christian communities, bishops taught summaries of Christian faith to new believers who confessed the faith at baptism. These local summaries of the gospel varied from place to place, but they were not widely divergent. All were expressions of a shared "Rule of Faith"—*regula fidei*—that provided the church with a norm of Christian faith and life.

As early as the second century, Tertullian provided a striking rendition of the already traditional Rule of Faith:

> The Rule of Faith—to state here and now what we maintain—is of course that by which we believe that there is but one God, who is none other than the Creator of the world, who produced everything from nothing through his Word, sent forth before all things; that this Word is called his Son, and in the name of God was seen in diverse ways by

the patriarchs, was ever heard in the prophets and finally was brought down by the Spirit and Power of God the Father into the Virgin Mary, was made flesh in her womb, was born of her and lived as Jesus Christ; who thereafter proclaimed a new law and a new promise of the kingdom of heaven, worked miracles, was crucified, on the third day rose again, was caught up into heaven and sat down at the right hand of the Father; that he sent in his place the power of the Holy Spirit to guide believers; that he will come again with glory to take the saints up into the fruition of the life eternal and the heavenly promises and to judge the wicked to everlasting fire, after the resurrection of both good and evil with the restoration of their flesh."[12]

Irenaeus also recounted an expression of the Rule of Faith. He concluded by commenting: "Having received this preaching and this faith, as I have said, the Church, although scattered in the whole world, carefully preserves it, as if living in one house. She believes these things [everywhere] alike, as if she had but one heart and one soul, and preaches them harmoniously, teaches them, and hands them down, as if she had but one mouth."[13] There is no doubt that Irenaeus painted an idealized portrait of the church's unanimity, but the early church did share substantial agreement about the shape of its faith. The Rule of Faith, expressed in teaching and summarized in baptismal confessions of faith, was both a digest of the story of God with us and the focal point of Christian identity. While the language varied from place to place, it summarized the same scriptural story and shared the same threefold structure.

The church's Rule of Faith was self-consciously biblical and consistently Trinitarian. It retained the narrative structure of Scripture in both liturgy and teaching, telling the story that summarized the gospel. This Rule of Faith—the story of God with us—is not merely a historical curiosity, for it remains present in current Christian worship. The Apostles' Creed, while not fixed in its precise form until the eighth century, is a version of the Rule of Faith that was used by the church in Rome as early as the second century. The Apostles' Creed is confessed regularly by contemporary congregations, continuing to form the faith of the church, and continuing to shape the church's vocation to "Go therefore and make disciples of all nations, baptizing them in the name of the Father and of the Son and of the Holy Spirit, and teaching them to obey everything that I have commanded you" (Matt. 28:19–20).

The early church's Rule of Faith was not the last word, however, for it left some things unsettled and ambiguous. Chief among the ambiguities that needed clarification were the relationships between the three main "characters" in the story: Father, Son, and Holy Spirit. In the early years of the fourth century the Christian church faced a crisis—a stark choice between two radically different interpretations of the Rule of Faith, two divergent readings of the scriptural narrative. On the one side, some Christians claimed that while the Son is the mediator between God and humankind, he is not truly God. The mediator is like God—more like God than any other being—but is not the same as God. They were sure that the one true God existed before the Son, which meant that the Son must be a created being, only derivatively divine. On the other side were Christians who declared that the Son is truly God, existent with the Father from all eternity. God is fully present in the Son, they said, making himself known in Jesus Christ.

It is not necessary to recount the details of the dispute or the history of the first great Ecumenical Council at Nicaea. The position of the second, "orthodox" group, prevailed. In the ensuing decades, the orthodox insight that the Son is of one being with the Father was broadened to encompass the unity of the Spirit with the Father and Son. The oneness of God, Father Son and Holy Spirit, was confessed by the church in the Nicene–Constantinopolitan Creed of 325/381, and has been confessed by the church through the centuries:

> We believe in one God,
> the Father, the Almighty,
> maker of heaven and earth,
> of all that is,
> seen and unseen.
>
> We believe in one Lord Jesus Christ,
> the only Son of God,
> eternally begotten of the Father,
> God from God, Light from Light,
> true God from true God,
> begotten, not made,
> of one being with the Father;
> through him all things were made. . . .

We believe in the Holy Spirit, the Lord, the giver of life,

who proceeds from the Father and the Son,

who with the Father and the Son is worshiped and glorified . . .[14]

Why was the issue of the full divinity of Son and Spirit with the Father a matter of such crucial importance that it nearly split the church? Why is it an issue that continues to perplex and even separate so many in the church? Would it not be simpler to proclaim one God alone with Jesus Christ and the Holy Spirit as God's aides, or as helpful pathways to God? What difference does it make to Christian faith and life whether we proclaim one God alone, with two divine assistants, or one God alone, Father Son and Holy Spirit?

The answer lies in the phrase of the Nicene Creed following the declaration that the Son is "of one being with the Father." The Creed proclaims the good news that all was "for us and for our salvation." The One who is God from God, light from light, true God from true God, *for us and for our salvation* . . .

. . . came down from heaven,

was incarnate of the Holy Spirit and the Virgin Mary

and became truly human.

For our sake he was crucified under Pontius Pilate;

He suffered death and was buried.

On the third day he rose again

in accordance with the Scriptures;

he ascended into heaven

and is seated at the right hand of the Father.

He will come again in glory to judge the living and the dead,

and his kingdom will have no end.

In the same way, *for us and for our salvation*, the Holy Spirit is the Lord and Giver of life,

who proceeds from the Father and the Son,

who with the Father and the Son is worshiped and glorified,

who has spoken through the prophets.

The Creed's declaration that all was "for us and for our salvation" makes it clear that the issue—then and now—cuts to the heart of Christian confidence in salvation and the integrity of Christian life. Can we believe that Christ is "true God" and therefore trust that the salvation announced and accomplished in Jesus Christ is God's gracious will? Or is Jesus Christ something less than God so that God's will remains an uncertain purpose behind, above, and beyond the words and deeds of Jesus Christ? Are men and women who are "in Christ" thereby reconciled to God? Or is there another step that must be taken in order to be reconciled to the still-hidden God who dwells behind Christ? Has God come to humankind in the person of Jesus Christ? Or does God remain aloof from us, only sending an emissary?

The unity of God, Father Son and Holy Spirit, is the essential guarantee that we are able to know God truly. If Jesus Christ is not "truly God" as well as "truly human," then he is merely an approach toward a remote god who remains essentially unknown and unknowable. Similarly, if "the Spirit" is not the Holy Spirit of God, then our deepest spiritual experience is not an encounter with the one true God, but only an approach to a mysterious god who remains effectively distant. Who is God, really? What is God like, truly? Our understanding and experience of God depend on our understanding and experience of Jesus Christ and of the Holy Spirit, which is to say our understanding and experience of the one God, Father Son and Holy Spirit.

We Believe in One True God

Christians confess faith in the one God who created all that is—heaven and earth, invisible reality as well as that which is accessible to the senses. The creating God is not like the "clockmaker" of deism, who set the world in motion and then left it to function on its own. Rather, the Creator is "the Almighty" who continues to enact providential care over all that is. Neither is this creating God a self-contained and self-sufficient monad. Rather, the Creator is "the Father," the essentially relational One whose loving providence in creation is exercised through the redemptive action of the Son and the Spirit.

Christians confess faith in the one Lord Jesus Christ, the Son who is of one being with the Father and through whom all was created. This Lord is not a distant cosmic ruler, but the Son who was sent by the Father in the power of the Holy Spirit. Jesus is Lord, present in our time and space for the sake of our salvation. Crucified, dead, risen, and ascended, this Jesus is Lord who will come again for the sake of the world and its salvation.

Christians confess faith in the Holy Spirit, the Lord and Giver of life. This Spirit is not a third-rate deity, but the Holy Spirit of God through whom the Son was incarnate. Neither is the Holy Spirit a vague spiritual presence, for the Spirit speaks through the prophets, makes us one with Christ in baptism and Eucharist, gathers and sends the church, and guarantees the life of the world that will come.

This one God is known to us through the narratives of Scripture and in our experience of the grace of the Lord Jesus Christ, the love of God, and the communion of the Holy Spirit. But are both the witness of Scripture and the experience of our lives true to who God is? Is the threefold way that God relates to us a true manifestation of who God is *as God*? The consistent Christian confession is that God's own being is not different from the biblical story of God or the church's continuing experience of God. As God is to us, so God truly is: self-giving, loving, a communion of life. The Trinitarian names we use for God—Father Son and Holy Spirit—express relationships within the One God: God is Father in relation to the Son, Son in relation to the Father, Spirit in the loving bond of the unity of Father and Son. Trinity is not philosophical speculation in search of reality. Trinity is the assurance that the God we know from the Scriptures and from the enduring experience of the community of faith, is who God really is. In Robert Jenson's striking formulation, "God is what happens between Jesus and his Father in their Spirit."[15]

God makes himself present to us as one God who is Father Son and Holy Spirit. "Unless we grasp these," says Calvin, "only the bare and empty name of God flits about in our brains, to the exclusion of the true God."[16] "God" can mean almost anything to anyone, but to know God's presence among us as Father Son and Holy Spirit is to know *this* God, not just any god. We cannot presume that our doctrine of the triune God is an exhaustive definition of "God as God is," for God remains free from the confines of human language, but we can be confident that God relates to us as God is.

Knowing that God's threefold relatedness to the world is the truth about the very being of God does more than get our doctrine straight. In confessing the triune being of God we find assurance that the life of God is not remote and inaccessible to us. God *is* self-giving, mutually affirming, community-building love. Thus, our experience of God's love is not simply an experience of something God does, but an experience of *God*. As God does, so God is. Moreover, since God is who God is *in relation to us*, we are invited to share in the very life of God as we live lives of self-giving, mutually affirming, community-building love.

Trinitarian understandings of God and God's Way in the world are radically different from every general idea about "divinity." Our understanding of God's *sovereignty* is changed from remote governance to loving care for all creation. God's *power* is transformed from the coercion of dominant force into the dynamic reign of loving relationship. God's *salvation* is no longer a legal transaction, but a gracious restoration of communion. God's *new community* is neither a collective nor an assemblage of individuals, but the presence of open mutuality. As God does, so God is—and so we together are invited to do and be as we share in the very life of God.

If we say that the Trinity remains a "mystery," it is not because God and God's Way are unfathomable. Rather, the more we know of the triune God, the more we are aware of how much more there is to "the depth of the riches and wisdom and knowledge of God" (Rom. 11:33). We can never fully comprehend God, but we are no longer locked in despair or imprisoned by arcane speculation, for God has disclosed his very self in his relationship with us. Our knowledge of this God is our relationship with "the one triune God, the Holy One of Israel, whom alone we worship and serve (A Brief Statement of Faith, lines 5–6)."

A Concluding Word about Language

Some readers will be appalled by the constant reliance on Father-Son-Spirit language in this discussion of the Trinity, and by the regular application to God of the pronouns *he* and *himself*. These are not two variants of a failure to use "inclusive language," but rather two different problems. Both are discussed briefly in the Introduction, but a few more words about Trinitarian language are called for in this chapter.

I do not use Father-Son language merely because it is scriptural and creedal language, although this is not an insignificant consideration. Scripture bears witness to Jesus, who is identified by the very voice of God: "You are my Son, the Beloved." Scripture bears witness to God who is identified by Jesus as "my Father." Moreover, the relationship is characterized in terms of mutual knowledge: "no one knows who the Son is except the Father, or who the Father is except the Son and anyone to whom the Son chooses to reveal him" (Luke 10:22). Throughout the centuries the creeds of the church have made consistent confession of One God, Father Son and Holy Spirit. Setting aside creed and Scripture—and, more important, setting aside the words of Jesus whom we confess to be God with us—is not something to be done lightly, however admirable the motivation.

The more important reason for retention of Father-Son-Spirit language—and perhaps the reason that occasioned it in the first place—is that the language is both relational and personal. Unlike, for example, "Creator, Redeemer, and Sustainer," Father-Son-Spirit language is relational. Fathers have sons, sons have fathers, fathers and sons have and are bound by spirit. On the other hand, Creators do not have redeemers, redeemers do not have creators, creators and redeemers do not have sustainers. Whatever language is used for Trinity, it must be relational. Similarly, language for Trinity must be personal. Rock, cornerstone, and temple are biblical images that, while suggesting a certain relationship, are impersonal.

Trinitarian language is not confined to Father-Son-Spirit language, however. A Presbyterian Church (U.S.A.) task force on the doctrine of the Trinity affirms the foundational language of Father-Son-Spirit, yet identifies other faithful articulations such as Speaker-Word-Breath, Sun-Ray-Warmth, and Giver-Gift-Giving. These and other images that express Trinity are valuable in particular theological and liturgical contexts, perhaps especially in hymnody and prayer. They are not meant as substitutes for Father-Son-Spirit, however, and do not as fully express the biblical narrative of salvation.

One final observation is in order. Father-Son-Spirit language is explicitly Trinitarian language, language that expresses Trinitarian relationships. It is not intended as pervasive and exclusive language for God. It is as inappropriate to address God exclusively as "Father" as it is to refer to Trinity as Creator-Redeemer-Sustainer. "Father" is the name used in relation to the Son, not a generic title for God. As we speak of the one triune God, rather than of the Trinitarian relations, we are freed to use language that expresses a range of biblical images. Long before "inclusive language" became an issue in the church, John Calvin noted that "God did not satisfy himself with proposing the example of a father, but in order to express his very strong affection, he chose to liken himself to a mother, and calls [the people of Israel] not merely 'children,' but *the fruit of the womb*, towards which there is usually a warmer affection."[17]

In theology and worship we are free to call upon the full range of biblical language for God, from fortress to mother hen, just as we are free to speak of Jesus Christ as the good shepherd and the Holy Spirit as the advocate. It is only when we speak of the Trinitarian reality that we are drawn inevitably to the scriptural truth that "God has sent the Spirit of his Son into our hearts, crying, 'Abba! Father!'" (Gal. 4:6).

Notes

1. Kathleen Norris, *Amazing Grace: A Vocabulary of Grace* (New York: Riverhead Books, 1998), pp. 290–291.
2. Ignaz Franz (attributed), "Holy God, We Praise Your Name," *The Presbyterian Hymnal* (Louisville: Westminster/John Knox Press, 1990), no. 460. (Hereafter *The Presbyterian Hymnal*.)
3. Tobias Clausnitzer, "We All Believe in One True God," *The Presbyterian Hymnal*, no. 137.
4. Karl Rahner, *The Trinity* (New York: Crossroad Publishing, 1997), pp. 10–11.
5. Catherine Mowry LaCugna, *God For Us: The Trinity and Christian Life* (New York: HarperSanFrancisco, 1991), p. 1.
6. Reginald Heber, "Holy, Holy, Holy! Lord God Almighty!" *The Presbyterian Hymnal*, no. 138.
7. Fred Pratt Green, "God Is Here!" *The Presbyterian Hymnal*, no. 461.
8. *Book of Common Worship*, Presbyterian Church (U.S.A.) (Louisville: Westminster/John Knox Press, 1993), p. 50. (Hereafter *Book of Common Worship*.)
9. Thomas Ken, "Praise God, from Whom All Blessings Flow," *The Presbyterian Hymnal* (Louisville: Westminster/John Knox Press, 1990), no. 593.
10. *Book of Common Worship*, p. 572.
11. Dietrich Ritschl, *Memory and Hope* (New York: Macmillan, 1967), p. 153.
12. Tertullian, *Prescriptions against Heretics 13*, in *Early Latin Theology*, ed. S. L. Greenslade (Philadelphia: Westminster Press, 1956), pp. 39–40.
13. Irenaeus, *Adversus Haereses* 1.10.2, in *Early Christian Fathers*, ed. Cyril C. Richardson (Philadelphia: Westminster Press, 1953), p. 360.
14. *The Book of Confessions*, 1.1–3.
15. Robert W. Jenson, "How Does Jesus Make a Difference?" in *Essentials of Christian Theology*, ed. William C. Placher (Louisville: Westminster John Knox Press, 2003), p. 196.
16. John Calvin, *Institutes of Christian Religion* 1.13.2; 2 vols., ed. John T. McNeill, trans. Ford Lewis Battles (Philadelphia: Westminster Press, 1/960), p. 122. (Hereafter *Institutes*.)
17. John Calvin, *Commentary on Isaiah* 49:15.

The Way, *The* Truth, *The* Life?

As a Parsi, Dr. Durawalla was descended from Persian Zoroastrians who had come to India in the seventh and eighth centuries to escape Muslim persecution. Farrokh's father, however, was such a virulent, ascerbic atheist that the doctor had never been a practicing Zoroastrian. And Farrokh's conversion to Christianity would doubtless have killed his godless father, except that his father was already dead; the doctor didn't convert until he was almost forty.

Because Dr. Durawalla was a Christian, his own mortal body would never be exposed to the Towers of Silence; but despite his father's inflammatory atheism, Farrokh respected the habits of his fellow Parsis and practicing Zoroastrians. . . .

—John Irving, *A Son of the Circus* [1]

The most dramatic feature of contemporary Christian existence in North America is the emergence of pervasive religious pluralism. An American society that was already in the process of separating itself from the influence of Christianity and its churches is now characterized by a profusion of religious options ranging from enduring traditions such as Islam, Buddhism, and Hinduism, to New Age spiritualities. When I was a boy growing up in Massachusetts, Hindus and Buddhists were confined to the pages of *National Geographic*. If anyone talked about marrying outside of one's faith, the issue was a Protestant marrying a Roman Catholic. There was little question, even among the many who were not faithful church members, that Christianity was "true," superior to all the "pagan" religions.

Now, everything has changed. Hindus and Buddhists and Muslims are no longer quaintly costumed people on magazine pages. They are our neighbors and coworkers, whose kids play soccer with our kids, and whose places of worship are in Kentucky and Wyoming as well as Jakarta and Bombay. The pluralism of the American religious scene flows beyond enduring faith traditions and organized religious communities into bookstore sections on Wicca and astrology, eco-spirituality and eclectic meditation techniques.

The most apparent reason for American religious pluralism is immigration. Reform of the immigration and naturalization laws, beginning in 1965, made possible a new wave of immigrants from Asia, Africa, South America, and the Middle East. As hundreds of thousands, then millions of people brought their religious faith with them to America, they were encountered by a once "Christian" nation that was already far down the road of secularization. More important, they were encountered by a Christianity that had been corroded by self-identification with the culture, confused by an inability to articulate the gospel clearly, weakened by waning confidence in its own truth, and burdened by a guilty conscience over a missionary history that at times was linked to governmental colonialism and cultural imperialism. All of this, coupled with American individualism that relegated religious faith to the realm of personal choice, made it difficult for American Christianity to understand its new context *theologically.*

The church's difficulty in responding to the new reality of pervasive pluralism has been exacerbated in recent decades by internal theological crises. There have been multiple challenges to the traditional assumption that a core of Christian faith was shared throughout the church. The life of the Christian community is not marked by common conviction, but by divisive debates about the emergence of feminist thought, the rise of the religious right, a range of sexuality issues, abortion, the relationship between science and Christian faith, and more. Hostile wrangling among contending groups within the church contributes to a loss of routine confidence in traditional authorities and weakened commitment to traditional truths. One result is that the Christian community is uncertain about how to understand the great world religions, puzzled by the emergence of nontraditional spiritualities, and ambivalent about the once certain affirmation that Jesus Christ is *the* way, *the* truth, and *the* life.

There is a sense in which our confusion about the relationship between Christian faith and other faiths is itself puzzling. After all, throughout most of its history Christian faith has lived within a context of religious pluralism. Indeed, fidelity to the one God—the God of Abraham, Isaac, and Jacob . . . the God who made himself known in Jesus Christ—has almost always been lived in the midst of multiple religions that provided numerous challenges, temptations, and seductions. Religious pluralism was a primary reality at the infancy both of Israel and of the church. Religious pluralism was a primary reality during critical formative stages both of Israel's faith and the church's faith. Outside of western Europe and North America, religious pluralism has been a primary reality for most Christians throughout history.

One God

Israel was called by the great *shema*, "Hear, O Israel, the LORD is our God, the LORD alone" (Deut. 6:4). And what is the first commandment that Israel was called to obey? "I am the LORD your God, who brought you out of the land of Egypt, out of the house of slavery; you shall have no other gods before me" (Ex. 20:2). This one-Godness of Israel's faith was more than a philosophical position. Israel knew that the Lord was a jealous God, requiring absolute loyalty. When Israel forgot, which it often did, prophets arose who called the people a whore, ridiculed the little gods made of wood and stone, and summoned the people back to exclusive faithfulness.

> My people consult a piece of wood,
>> and their divining rod gives them oracles.
> For a spirit of whoredom has led them astray,
>> and they have played the whore, forsaking their God. . . .
> Return, O Israel, to the LORD your God,
>> for you have stumbled because of your iniquity.
>
> (Hosea 4:12; 14:1)

The earliest Christian community flourished in a Hellenistic culture that was wildly religious: Greek gods, Roman gods, and Egyptian gods . . . magic societies and mystery cults . . . emperor worship and local shrines. The Greco-Roman world encompassed a bewildering mass of religious options. Persons had a wide range of spiritual choices, and were quite comfortable in embracing more than one. Hellenistic culture dealt with the questions posed by religious pluralism by denying that the concept of particular identity could apply to God, thus allowing multiple identities to apply to the general concept of god. Into this mélange of spirituality Christians proclaimed the startling message of one God, Savior and Lord.

The Christian proclamation was presented as Good News, a gospel of liberation from the tyranny of fickle gods, freedom from "the elemental spirits of the universe." Paul voiced the truth of Christ that was shared by all who were in Christ: "We know that 'an idol has no real existence,' and that 'there is no God but one.' For although there may be so-called gods in heaven or on earth—as indeed there are many 'gods' and many 'lords'—yet for us there is one God, the Father, from whom are all things and for whom we exist, and one Lord, Jesus Christ, through whom are all things and through whom we exist" (1 Cor. 8:4–6, RSV). Even so, the profusion of surrounding religions and their capricious gods remained a danger. Religious systems for controlling life, ranging from astrology through spiritual techniques to secret rites, were tempting options in a confusing world. "Formerly, when you did not know God"—Paul wrote to wavering Christians—"you were enslaved to beings that by nature are not gods. Now, however, that you have come to know God, or rather to be known by God, how can you turn back again . . . ?" (Gal. 4:8–9). The one God, Father Son and Holy Spirit, brought liberation from the old, discredited Greek and Roman gods, and from the new, exciting mystery cults, and from the everyday gods of petty fortune. But these spiritual prisons remained strangely seductive, and so Christians were called to "stand firm" and "not submit again to a yoke of slavery" (Gal. 5:1).

The pages of our Bible seem unambiguous: there is but one God, made known in Jesus Christ, present to us now in the Holy Spirit. All other gods are either the projections of human dream-wishes or enslaving fictions spun by the principalities and powers. In any event, the lures of false gods are to be rejected. Christian fidelity to the one God and rejection of other, false 'gods' and 'lords' was not a first-century idiosyncrasy, confined to the pages of the Bible. Throughout the centuries the church's testimony has been unambiguous:

> We believe in one God, the Father, the Almighty . . .
> We believe in one Lord, Jesus Christ, the only Son of God . . .
> We believe in the Holy Spirit, . . . who with the Father and
> the Son is worshiped and glorified . . .
>
> (Nicene Creed, fourth century)

We confess and acknowledge one God alone, to whom
alone we must cleave, whom alone we must serve, whom
only we must worship, and in whom alone we put our trust.
(Scots Confession, sixteenth century)

[W]e trust in the one triune God, the Holy One of Israel,
whom alone we worship and serve.
(A Brief Statement of Faith, twentieth century)

Truth and Truths

Many contemporary American Christians are likely to affirm that while
the Bible and the creeds may be true for Christians, they are not
necessarily true for everyone. The gospel of Jesus Christ may be the
truth, but not necessarily the *whole* truth and *nothing but* the truth.
"Surely," some Christians say, "God is beyond our human concepts so
that all religions contain some measure of truth and no one religion is
truth's exclusive possessor. Surely each religion is a possible pathway
to God. Wouldn't it be arrogant for Christians to claim that they alone
know the truth about God, that they alone worship God in spirit and
in truth, and that they alone are favored by God? Christian faith may
be *our* faith, but it cannot be the only worthwhile or valid faith, can it?"

This leads other Christians to react with firm assertions of the truth
of Christian faith. "Surely," they say, "the Bible is revelation of the one
and only God and the historic creeds are reliable expressions of
universal truth. Because God is beyond all human concepts we must
look to the revealed truth of the gospel, rejecting the false claims of all
religion. Wouldn't it be arrogant to substitute American middle-class
tolerance for God's revelation? People of other faiths may be sincere,
moral, exemplary people, but they are wrong about God and their faith
is misplaced."

In short, there is disagreement among us, *theological* disagreement
within the Christian community that results in the intensification of
church fights and debilitation of the church's mission. These
theological disagreements are not peripheral matters that can be
ignored by most Christians, however, for they are about the heart of
the gospel. Disagreements about core issues of faith are more than
theoretical disputes among theologians, or complicated controversies

among ministers. The way we deal with core issues of Christian faith shapes our experience of church life every week. The way we think about foundational matters shapes worship, determines what is taught to children and youth, sets the tone of congregational and personal evangelism, and marks the direction and form of mission in the world.

The reality of religious pluralism and our theological responses are complex matters that require close reading of the Scriptures, attentive listening to the wisdom of the Christian tradition, careful analysis of the culture, and faithful thinking about the grace of the Lord Jesus Christ, the love of God, and the communion of the Holy Spirit. While all of this requires more time and thought than most people can give, as a community of faith the church must strive to gain some clarity about the issue as well as a measure of confidence about faith's affirmations.

Christian Faith and Other Faiths

The first step in a theological approach to the relationship between Christian faith and other living faiths is the recognition that there is no actual religion, no reality called "other faiths." We are not dealing with a homogenized religious reality, but with the particularities of specific faiths. We do not encounter "other faiths," but we do encounter Judaism, Islam, Hinduism, and Buddhism . . . and also Baha'i, Jain, and Sikh . . . and also Confucianism and Shinto . . . and also Santeria, Rastafaria, and animism. Not only is there no monolithic reality, "other faiths," there is no possibility of limiting the particularity of specific faiths to the so-called "great religions." Who is to say that only the nice, sophisticated religions are worthy of our attention while religions that offend refined sensibilities are beyond the pale?

We cannot talk generically about Christianity and "other faiths," but only about the specific relationships between Christian faith and a range of other particular faiths.

Christianity and Judaism: From Calvin on, the Reformed tradition has understood God's covenant with Israel as inviolable. In fact, there is only one covenant of grace in which Israel and the church are embraced. Thus, the Christian church is spoken of as Israel's "younger brother," the branch grafted onto the tree.

Christianity and Islam: Islam is radically monotheistic: "There is no God but Allah and Mohammed is his prophet." Christianity, Judaism, and Islam share the conviction that there is but one God, a common forebear in Abraham, and a common reverence for "the Book."

Christianity and departures from Christianity: The most obvious instance is Mormonism, an offshoot from Christian faith that assumes a new revelation in additional scriptures. The new revelation leads to a new theism that maintains monotheistic language while positing a system of demigods.

Christianity and theistic religions: Prominent among the theistic "great religions" is polytheistic, pantheistic, sometimes henotheistic Hinduism. The absence of specific dogmas and tenets results in great diversity within Hinduism, which has been described as an "encyclopedia of all religions."[2]

Christianity and non-theistic religions: Some forms of Buddhism acknowledge an unknowable deity, but classic Buddhism is nontheistic, a religion without a deity. No form of Buddhism has a personal concept of God.

Christianity and the religions of "spirits": Some indigenous African and Caribbean religions see the world as the playground of innumerable spirits who can be influenced ritually in order to avoid harm or win favor.

Christianity and religion-like cultural and ethical systems: Confucianism and Shinto are nontheistic, this-world-oriented ways of ordering family, society, and nation.

Even a superficial glance at some of the world's religious and ethical communities is enough to show that the issue is not simply "Christianity and other religions," but "Christianity and many other specific religious faiths." Religious pluralism is a complex reality that requires more than superficial tolerance or facile acceptance of multiple truths. Each particular religion has particular ways of answering basic questions: Who is God, really? Who are we, honestly? What does God have to do with us? What do we have to do with each other?

The answers given by various religions are not necessarily—in fact, not often—congruous. They are not consonant with Christian faith, and they are not consistent with each other. If Christianity, Islam, Buddhism, and all other religious faiths are alternative ways of understanding "god," then "god" is utterly unknown and unknowable. If they are different pathways to "god," then "god" is unreachable. The gods of multiple religious faiths are so wildly different from one another, and the pathways offered are so disparate, that even the concept "god" is illusive. Christian faith gives answers to basic theological questions that are different from the answers of other faiths. It is not even necessary to believe that Christian answers are true and other answers false in order to recognize the differences and to acknowledge their disparity. The reality of fundamental difference is apparent in a few brief illustrations.

Who is God? Both Christianity and Islam are monotheistic faiths, professing that there is but one God and that all other gods are false idols. But the character of the one God is understood quite differently by the two faiths. Christian faith in the one triune God—Father Son and Holy Spirit—is an affirmation that communion, relationship, is at the very heart of who God is, and at the very heart of how God acts to forge bonds of communion with humankind. For Muslims, Allah is an essentially impersonal God manifested as will and precept. The appropriate human response is submission and obedience. Thus, a "Muslim" is one who "surrenders" his or her whole being to Allah. The shape of surrender is found in the Five Pillars of Islam: *shahada*, the foundational creed that there is no God but Allah, and Mohammed is his prophet; *salat*, prescribed daily prayers; *zakat*, almsgiving; *sieyam*, fasting; and *hajj*, the pilgrimage to Mecca. The profound dedication of Muslims testifies to the power of Islam's message and the depth of its spiritual significance. Yet Christians and Muslims have very different understandings of who God/Allah is.

Who are we? Christianity and Buddhism have vastly dissimilar understandings of human being, human nature, and human purpose. For Christian faith, human persons are created by God, and so are created for communion with God, with other persons, and with all of creation. Life is God's good gift. Although human persons break communion with God, with each other, and with the earth and its creatures, salvation is God's creation of new communion through the incarnation, life, death, resurrection, and ascension of the Person, Jesus Christ. The "Four Noble Truths" of the Buddha understand human life differently. The essence of human life is pain, resulting from human desire, hatred, and blindness. Craving for life must be stilled by eliminating the desires that bind humans to earthly things and by achieving the knowledge through deaths and rebirths. The cessation of pain as the result of the cessation of craving brings a human to Nirvana, a state of total peace of soul and indifference to pleasure and pain. Nirvana is achieved through the Eightfold Way—practices of meditation and knowledge. Buddhist insights and practices show the way to a striking spirituality. Yet Christians and Buddhists have a very different understanding of human life.

What does God have to do with us? Christian faith believes that the love of the one God overflows to bathe creation and cleanse humankind. This overflowing love of God is expressed in the Father's sending of the Son in the power of the Holy Spirit to redeem the fallen world and to create new communion between God and humankind. Hinduism, on the other hand, encompasses a profusion of gods whose relationships to humans are diverse and contradictory. For instance, Siva is a god of fertility and destruction while Vishnu is pleasant and kindly. Brahma is a transcendent world soul while Durga, Kali, and Shakti are cruel goddesses. These and all the other gods have numerous avatars, or incarnations. Human life, then, is a perplexing labyrinth in which various gods are mollified and entreated in order that people may live out a favorable karma that will assure a better reincarnation. Hindu understanding of the gods and their relationships to human persons is complex and sophisticated, but it is very different from the Christian discernment of God's Way with humankind.

What do we have to do with each other? Christians understand that human beings are called to relationships of love and justice among persons and communities, groups and classes, races and nations. Love of neighbor is paired with love of God in a life of enduring communion.

This briefest of glances at other religious faiths does not pretend to be an adequate analysis of their beliefs and practices or even an elementary exercise in comparative religions. Its only purpose is to show that Christian faith and other living faiths differ from one another on basic religious questions. To blend all religious faiths into a general God-consciousness, or to imagine that all have the same end and all take us to the same god dishonors them all—Judaism, Hinduism, Buddhism, and Islam—as well as Christianity.

A Christian Ethic of Religious Pluralism

To be a Christian (or a Muslim or a Hindu) does not mean believing that other religious faiths and their adherents are to be dismissed, demeaned, or mistreated. To proclaim the truth of Christian faith (or Judaism or Buddhism) does not mean that other religious faiths are utterly false, misleading, and harmful. Too often, North American Christians disparage the traditions and beliefs of others. We may be insufficiently aware that religious pluralism is not new in the world, and not new to the Christian church. Only the North American experience of religious pluralism is new. We are able to draw on the Christian wisdom of other times and different places in order to form and live a Christian ethic of religious pluralism. A simple ethic of religious pluralism emerges from Christian faith itself.

First, Christians are called to treat persons of other faiths decently, as human beings deserving of respect and high human dignity. Muslims and Jews, Sikhs and Rastafarians are not to be ridiculed or avoided, much less mistreated or persecuted. Granting dignity and respect is more than bourgeois civility and cultural tolerance. For Christians, it is a gospel imperative. We are commanded to love God and neighbors. It is worth remembering that the first answer to the question, "Who is my neighbor?" was answered by presenting us with a heterodox, mixed-race foreigner! (Luke 10:29–37).[3]

Second, Christians are called to treat the religious faith and practice of others with respect. The beliefs of others are not to be caricatured or derided, but understood and honored. Their religious practices are not to be mocked or dismissed, but acknowledged and held in regard.

Third, Christians are called to engage in serious, genuine dialogue with people of other faiths, and to be open to the fruits of dialogue in which we can learn about and learn from other religious traditions. Christians are not Muslims, but we may be able to (re)learn from Islam something about the dynamics of obedience to God and the importance of communal disciplines. Christians are not Buddhists, but we may be able to (re)learn from Buddhism something about the destructive dynamics of worldly desire. Dialogue is a high form of respect for persons of other faiths, their beliefs and practices. It is not limited to giving and receiving information, but opens all participants to transformation.

Finally, Christians should bear witness to the gospel. Faithful witness, authentic proclamation of the truth of Christ in deeds and in words, must always be both truthful and modest, however. Acts of Christian love cannot be Trojan horses for aggressive proselytism, and words of Christian proclamation cannot be used as weapons to coerce conversion. Inaction and silence are not Christian options, however. Lack of Christian engagement in instances of human need and lack of Christian conviction in speech do not honor people of other faiths. We should always be prepared to give "an accounting for the hope that is in [us]; yet do it with gentleness and reverence" (1 Peter 3:15–16).

A Christian Theology of Religious Pluralism

North American Christians are only beginning to understand religious pluralism theologically. The churches must devote significant time and effort to thinking and discussing the way in which we understand the place of the world's religions in the love, grace, and communion of God. However, a Christian theology of religious pluralism starts from confidence in the veracity of Christian faith, an assurance that the gospel—the good news of God and God's Way in the world—is true. Confidence in the truth of the gospel is not rigid certainty that every articulation of Christian doctrine is wholly true while all convictions of other religious faiths are riddled with error. Yet Christian thinking about other living faiths can begin from confidence in the Christian account of who God is, who we are, what God has to do with us, and what we have to do with each other.

In 2002 the General Assembly of the Presbyterian Church (U.S.A.) affirmed a theological statement prepared by the church's Office of Theology and Worship. *Hope in the Lord Jesus Christ* sets out in summary form the good news that Jesus Christ is the Way (in the first instance, God's Way to us, and then God's Way with us, and only then our way to God), that Jesus Christ is the Truth (the disclosure of truth about God and about us), and that Jesus Christ is the Life (God's gift of a new Way of living this life and the sure hope of life's fulfillment in the presence of God). *Hope in the Lord Jesus Christ* then sets forth central affirmations of the story that narrates Christian truth:

> *Incarnation:* "Jesus Christ came to us as one of us, sharing our joy and sorrow. He proclaimed God's love, healed the sick, and was a friend of sinners. He continues to reveal God's gracious love, he is among us now, and he is still the friend of sinners. Jesus Christ was and is one with us in life; Jesus Christ was and is one with us in suffering and death. The Lord and Savior is Christ crucified, in whom God's weakness is stronger than human strength and God's foolishness is wiser than human wisdom."[4]

> *Crucifixion:* "The cross of Christ is at the heart of our faith, for it is through the Lord's death that we receive new life. The gospel of Christ crucified is a treasure that surpasses human language, and so the Bible displays a wealth of expression that leads us to thankful knowledge and grateful faith."[5]

> *Resurrection:* "Jesus Christ is with us in life and death. But death is not the last word, for God has raised him from the dead and exalted him above all rule and authority and power and dominion. The risen Christ is the living Lord of the cosmos. 'in Christ God was reconciling the world to himself' [2 Cor. 5:19]. For the sake of the world, the Word became flesh, for the sake of the world Jesus Christ lived among us, was crucified and raised from the dead. For the sake of the world Christ ascended to heaven, and for the sake of the world Christ will come again. All of this is God's good pleasure set forth in Christ 'as a plan for the fullness

of time, to gather up all things in him, things in heaven and things on earth' [Eph. 1:10]"[6]

If this is a true account—the truth about what happened and the meaning of what happened—then we must say that Christian faith proclaims Truth and that other accounts by other religious traditions are, in crucial respects, not the truth. This is not an arrogant claim or a dismissive judgment, and certainly not a hostile declaration. It is simply a recognition of the incompatibility of differing beliefs. God is not both personal *and* impersonal, self-giving *and* inaccessible. Human life is not both part of God's good creation *and* pain-filled craving that must be denied. God is not both loving redeemer *and* multiple divinities who work both goodness *and* destruction.

If the Christian account of what happened in Christ, and the meaning of what happened, is true, then Jesus Christ is God's Way to humankind. God has chosen to bring about salvation—the new creation of communion between God and humankind, and of communion among human beings—through Jesus Christ. In the words of the Second Helvetic Confession, "We teach and believe that this Jesus Christ our Lord is the unique and eternal Savior of the human race, and thus of the whole world, in whom by faith are saved all who before the law, under the law, and under the Gospel were saved, and however many will be saved at the end of the world"[7]

Who Then Can Be Saved?

The question of the truth of Christian faith is often confused with the question of who can be saved: only Christians? or also sincere, good people of other faiths? If Christian faith gives a true account of God and God's Way in the world, does it follow that explicit faith in Christ is a necessary prerequisite to salvation? Is overt belief, trust, and loyalty to Jesus Christ necessary to establish communion with God and communion among people? Christians differ on this question, but the Reformed tradition has always been clear that salvation is a consequence of God's grace, not the result of our faith. If we were saved by our own faith, then we would be our own saviors and God would be the recipient of *our* favor! In commenting on Ephesians 2:8 ("For by grace you have been saved through faith, and this is not your own doing; it is the gift of God") Calvin makes it clear that salvation is God's doing, not ours:

On the one side we must look at God, and, on the other, at man. God declares that he owes us nothing, so that salvation is not a reward or recompense, but unmixed grace. The next question is, in what way do men receive that salvation which is offered to them by the hand of God? The answer is, *by faith*; and hence he concludes that nothing connected with it is our own. If, on the part of God, it is grace alone, and if we bring nothing but faith, which strips us of all condemnation, it follows that salvation does not come from us.[8]

Salvation comes through grace alone, and God's grace engenders the response of faith—faith as trust and loyalty as well as belief—so that God's grace accomplishes the restoration of the full communion which is God's gracious will. Human faith is lived gratitude for the grace of the Lord Jesus Christ, the love of God, and the communion of the Holy Spirit. In faith we enter into the fullness of communion, but our faith does not engender God's grace, nor is our faith necessary in order to make God's grace effective.

Faith is the appropriate and ordinary reception of God's grace, but God's grace is not dependent on faith's reception. Thus, "The proclamation of the gospel for the salvation of humankind" is the church's first great purpose, calling people to life within new communion between God and humankind and among persons. Human faith and faithfulness is the form of salvation's lived reality, the primary mode of salvation's restored communion between God and ourselves, and the possibility of restored communion among ourselves.

Yet two crucial questions remain: (1) Do all who profess Jesus Christ as Lord and Savior truly receive God's gracious salvation? (2) Do some/all who do not profess Jesus Christ as Lord and Savior receive God's gracious salvation? On these questions the Reformed tradition has always evidenced a certain "agnosticism" (literally, "not knowing"), a modest unwillingness to make firm and certain judgments.

Do all who profess Jesus Christ as Lord and Savior receive God's gracious salvation? We sense, intuitively, that not all persons who profess faith are truly and surely persons of faith and faithfulness. Yet when confirmation class teenagers say the right words, and people transferring membership from other congregations present the right credentials, we do not presume to judge the sincerity or adequacy of their profession. Does this mean that every teenager's beliefs and loyalties are fully shaped by trust in Christ? Are all new members loyal to the Christ in whom they believe, shaping their lives by trust in him? For that matter, does every member of the church trust in "the Holy

Spirit, the Lord, the giver of life," believe in "one Lord, Jesus Christ," who "for us and for our salvation . . . came down from heaven, was incarnate of the Holy Spirit and the Virgin Mary," and trust in "one God, the Father, the Almighty, maker of heaven and earth"?

"Decisions for Christ" come in great variety. How can anyone know, really know, that another has made the decision, really made it? The only one who is in a position to make judgments regarding the adequacy of response is Jesus Christ, "and Christ died for us, Christ rose for us, Christ reigns in power for us, Christ prays for us" (Rom. 8:34, Phillips). That is why Calvin is insistent that "as regards justification, faith is something merely passive, bringing nothing of ours to the recovering of God's favor but receiving from Christ that which we lack.[9]

Do some/all who do not profess Jesus Christ as Lord and Savior receive God's gracious salvation? Just as we do not judge every profession of faith, we do not presume to judge that all who have not made a public profession of faith are outside the circle of God's grace. God's grace is not constrained by human response, and human response is not confined to precise articulations. Calvin addresses the question of apparent faith and its seeming absence:

> [D]aily events themselves remind us how far [God's] secret
> judgments surpass our comprehension. For those who
> seemed utterly lost and quite beyond hope are by [God's]
> goodness called back to the way, while those who more
> than others seemed to stand firm often fall. Therefore,
> according to God's secret predestination (as Augustine says),
> "many sheep are without, and many wolves are within." For
> [God] knows and has marked those who know neither him
> nor themselves. Of those who openly wear his badge, his
> eyes alone see the ones who are unfeignedly holy and will
> persevere to the very end—the ultimate point of salvation.[10]

God's "secret judgments" are beyond our capacity to determine, and so it is appropriate for us to refrain from confident assertions about the extent of God's grace. It may be helpful to point to a clear instance of Presbyterian "agnosticism" regarding those who have not made a profession of faith. The "Declaratory Statement" to the Westminster Confession of Faith deals with the matter of those who die in infancy: "[W]ith reference to Chapter X, Section 3, of the Confession of Faith ["Of Effectual Calling"], . . . it is not to be regarded as teaching that any who die in infancy are lost. We believe that all dying in infancy are included in the election of grace, and are regenerated and saved by Christ through the Spirit, who works when and where and how he pleases."[11] The Declaratory Statement does not answer all questions, for the salvation of infants is but one of many difficult cases concerning those who are not able to hear and respond to the gospel. For instance, what is counted as "infancy" and when does it end? What of persons with severe or profound mental retardation? And, of course, there is the perennial youth group question about those who have never heard the good news of Christ, and so have had no opportunity to make a profession of faith. Perhaps most difficult is the unsettling question of persons who have been unable to hear the good news of Christ because of the church's corruption. In all these matters, we do well to refrain from the presumption that we know the mind of God, trusting instead in "the doctrine that God desires not the death of any sinner, but has provided in Christ a salvation sufficient for all, adapted to all, and freely offered in the gospel to all."[12]

Hope in the Lord Jesus Christ affirms the Christian imperative to proclaim the gospel while expressing appropriate modesty about our knowledge of the scope of God's grace:

> Jesus Christ is the only Savior and Lord, and all people everywhere are called to place their faith, hope, and love in him. No one is saved by virtue of inherent goodness or admirable living, for 'by grace you have been saved through faith, and this is not your own doing; it is the gift of God' (Ephesians 2:8). No one is saved apart from God's gracious redemption in Jesus Christ. Yet we do not presume to limit the sovereign freedom of 'God our Savior, who desires everyone to be saved and to come to the knowledge of the truth' (1 Timothy 2:4). Thus, we neither restrict the grace of God to those who profess explicit faith in Christ nor assume that all people are saved regardless of faith. Grace, love, and communion belong to God, and are not ours to determine.[13]

The church's statement is genuinely agnostic: It only states what we do not presume to know, placing trust in God alone. It concerns only *explicit* profession of faith, not the response of faith to God's grace, which is known to God alone.

Is salvation in Christ alone? Does no one come to the Father but through him?

Yes!

Is explicit profession of faith required to be embraced by the grace of the Lord Jesus Christ, the love of God, and the communion of the Holy Spirit? (Or, put crudely, are only Christians saved?)

NO! The Presbyterian Church's *Study Catechism* puts the matter well:

Q. 49. Will all human beings be saved?

No one will be lost who can be saved. The limits to salvation, whatever they may be, are known only to God. Three truths above all are certain. God is a holy God who is not to be trifled with. No one will be saved except by grace alone. And no judge could possibly be more gracious than our Lord and Savior, Jesus Christ.[14]

Notes

1. John Irving, *A Son of the Circus* (New York: Random House, 1994), p. 11.
2. *Polytheism* is the worship of many gods. *Pantheism* is the belief that the laws and powers of the universe are divine. *Henotheism* is the worship of one God while recognizing other gods.
3. *Heterodoxy* is deviation from orthodox, or traditional, standards.
4. *Hope in the Lord Jesus Christ,* Presbyterian Church (U.S.A.) (Louisville: Office of Theology and Worship, 2002), lines 101–110, p. 10.
5. Ibid., lines 117–122, p. 10.
6. Ibid., lines 134–147, p. 11.
7. Second Helvetic Confession, *The Book of Confessions*, 5.007.
8. John Calvin, *Commentary on the Epistle to the Ephesians*, trans. William Pringle (Grand Rapids: Baker Book House, 1993), p. 227.
9. Calvin, *Institutes* 3.13.5, p. 768.
10. Calvin, *Institutes* 4.1.8, p. 1022.
11. Westminster Confession of Faith, *BC*, 6.193.
12. Ibid., 6.192.
13. *Hope in the Lord Jesus Christ*, lines 155–168, pp.11–12.
14. *The Study Catechism: Full Version,* Presbyterian Church (U.S.A.) (Louisville: Witherspoon Press, 1998), p. 30.

The Church

"Ian, have you fallen into the hands of some *sect*?" his father asked.

"No, I haven't," Ian said. "I have merely discovered a church that makes sense to me, the same as Dober Street Presbyterian makes sense to you and Mom."

"Dober Street didn't ask us to abandon our educations," his mother told him. "Of course we have nothing against religion; we raised all of you children to be Christians. But *our* church never asked us to abandon our entire way of life."

"Well, maybe it should have," Ian said.

—Anne Tyler, *Saint Maybe*[1]

The preservation of the truth is a great end of the *church*. At first glance it may seem strange to entrust the truth of the gospel to the church. Trusting the church may seem even stranger after a second and third glance, for the church we know is an improbable guardian of the gospel. Its history contains more than a measure of misjudgment, error, falsehood, and deceit. On a smaller scale, denominations and congregations, even at their best, are a blend of gospel truth and self-serving deception. Admittedly, preservation of the truth is the church's *calling*, not its alleged accomplishment. Even so, it may be asking too much to expect the church to bear responsibility for the conservation of evangelical truth.

The church's all-too-human frailty was set out in bold relief by the remarkable prayers of confession offered by Pope John Paul II in March 2000. Following an invitation to repentance, and a Confession of Sins in General, prayers were prayed in "Confession of Sins Committed in the Service of Truth." First, Cardinal Ratzinger called on all to pray:

Let us pray that each one of us, looking to the Lord Jesus, meek and humble of heart, will recognize that even men of the Church, in the name of faith and morals, have sometimes used methods not in keeping with the Gospel in the solemn duty of defending the truth.

Following a time of silent prayer, the Holy Father prayed:

Lord, God of all men and women, in certain periods of history Christians have at times given in to intolerance and have not been faithful to the great commandment of love, sullying in this way the face of the Church, your Spouse. Have mercy on your sinful children and accept our resolve to seek and promote truth in the gentleness of charity, in the firm knowledge that truth can prevail only in virtue of truth itself. We ask this through Christ our Lord.

Then came the ancient chant, *Kyrie, eleison; Kyrie, eleison; Kyrie, eleison.* Lord, have mercy, indeed. The Pope's prayers were a moving act of repentance and contrition that all Christians could pray. Yet the prayers themselves, and the discussion surrounding them, point to the difficulty we have with the very concept of "church." Was the prayer confessing the sin of the church, or only the sins of some intolerant and faithless church members in certain times and places? Does the church always preserve the truth even when some of its members make errors in the service of truth? If some members sin, but the church does not, what do we mean by "church" apart from its members? And if the truth is to be preserved, what do we mean by "church" as the agent of its protection?

What Is the Church?

Church is an elastic word that can be stretched or contracted to include a lot or a little. The problem is that we are never clear what is meant when the word is uttered. Does *church* mean *the one holy catholic and apostolic church* of the Creed? *All Christians everywhere?* The *communion of saints?* A denomination such as the *Presbyterian Church (U.S.A.)?* The local *First Presbyterian Church?* The *true believers* within a mixed church? Or does *church* mean something either more abstract or more concrete than any of these? Even if we mean all of these things at one time or another, how do we know for sure what is meant at any given time? And what do we make of the tensions among various shades of meaning?

Theological talk about the church may be especially perplexing. What *church* is meant by statements such as, "In the power of the Holy Spirit the church experiences itself as the messianic fellowship of service for the kingdom of God in the world"[2] and "[the church] therefore sees itself and its powers and tasks as deriving from and existing in the eschatological history of the Spirit."[3] Do actual denominations and congregations see themselves that way? Probably not or, to the extent that they do, it is only in a mirror dimly. Too much theological exploration of the church falls into a pattern of talking about an ideal as if it were the actual community of faith.

Inflated rhetoric about ecclesial ideals may be intended to inspire the actual church to reform its life in correspondence to the perfect paradigm, but the result is less salutary. Talking about an ideal as if it were the *real* church creates a gap between it and the actual church we experience. The gap between ideal and actual often leads to scorn for the modest reality that so clearly fails to live up to lovely theological yarns about the church as messianic fellowship, the church as *koinonia*, the church as perichoretic Trinitarian community, the church as participant in the holiness of God, the church as the proleptic expression of restored humanity, and so on.[4-6]

Not surprisingly, the gap between the ideal church and the actual church leads some ministers and members to hold the actual church in contempt. Careless use of idealistic concepts contributes greatly to the disparagement of the church. For some, this takes the form of abandoning an actual congregation in order to search for a better version. For others, it takes the form of rejecting a flawed denomination in favor of a purer model. Countless others leave the failed church altogether. Yet even those who remain in the actual church are not immune to the harm done by idealistic notions of the "true church." Since the actual never measures up, discouragement is often the order of the day.

Mere empirical description of the church does not seem much better, however. There is some advantage to concentrating on the actual church rather than a theological ideal, but description of the way things are may lead to contentment with the institutional status quo, or become confused with organizational prescriptions for capitalizing on the current state of society. Religious bookstores are full of "how-to" manuals for the church that make a virtue of sociological necessity. For instance, the observation that most American congregations are homogeneous with regard to race, class, and other social indicators often leads to evangelism and outreach strategies that seek to capitalize on demographic realities. Descriptions of the characteristics of various "generations" may lead to conforming church life to meet consumer preference. Much of this exploration views the actual church as if it were the expression of the church's calling: "As the social demographics of religious constituencies change over time, religious and spiritual leaders are in positions to envision beliefs and practices appropriate to changing circumstances. In recent times especially, religious messages and practices have come to be frequently restylized, made to fit a target clientele . . ."[7] We need a way to understand "church" that avoids the pitfalls of abstract idealism and social determinism. The way forward begins with a focus on congregations.

Where Is the Church?

Lutheran theologian Gordon Lathrop provides a way of talking about the church that preserves its actual existence without abandoning its theological character. Lathrop centers on congregations rather than on abstract universals or on denominations, but his congregational concentration moves beyond generalities. Lathrop focuses on the central act of the community of faith: the congregation assembled for worship. As he begins his exploration of the church, Lathrop notes that "*church* will be understood here primarily as *assembly*. Church will be seen as a gathering of people to do those central things that identify them as Christian. It will be understood as the concrete meetings-for-worship we do really know."[8] Lathrop's "liturgical ecclesiology" reflects on the actual assembly's actual worship to assess such things as the church's well-being, unity, and relevance. His approach seems intuitively right, for it corresponds to the central element in our weekly experience of the church. The approach seems analytically right as well, avoiding both idealism and cynicism. *Church* as *assembly* is not a theological abstraction because it can be discussed by concrete reference to what actually happens when the assembly gathers for worship. Yet *church* as *assembly* is not mere sociological description because the assembly gathers in more or less faithful response to what God has done and its worship is directed more or less faithfully toward God.

Lathrop's focus on the worshiping congregation as the basic form of church affects the way we think about the Great Ends of the Church. While the preservation of the truth is the church's calling in all expressions of the church and in all church institutions, it is primarily the responsibility of the assembly to preserve the truth of the gospel! Surely presbyteries and seminaries and the General Assembly bear responsibility for the truth, but these bodies only serve to assist worshiping churches as they hear and proclaim the truth, confess and pray the truth, celebrate and serve the truth. If the primary form of church is the worshiping assembly, all of the Great Ends of the Church are the primary calling of the worshiping assembly. Proclamation of the gospel for the salvation of humankind . . . shelter, nurture, and spiritual fellowship of the children of God . . . maintenance of divine worship . . . preservation of the truth . . . promotion of social righteousness . . . exhibition of the kingdom of heaven to the world: these are first and foremost the purposes of each Christian congregation, and, first and foremost, they are located and lived as the congregation assembles for worship.

Lathrop's liturgical ecclesiology is not a modern innovation. Focus on the worshiping assembly recovers a central insight of sixteenth-century reformers Martin Luther and John Calvin. Calvin's identification of the church is well known: "Wherever we see the Word of God purely preached and heard, and the sacraments administered according to Christ's institution, there, it is not to be doubted, a church of God exists."[9] Preaching and hearing, Baptism and the Lord's Supper—these "marks of the church" are marks of the congregation assembled in worship. Thus, gospel proclamation and response in word and sacrament should not be confused with doctrinal purity or precise thinking about the sacraments. Calvin's marks point us to worshiping congregations, not classrooms, studies, or libraries.

The church in sixteenth-century Geneva was very different from the church in twenty-first-century North America. Calvin's insights are not necessarily time-bound, however. We may profit from listening to the way he thought through the matter.

A Church of the Word and Sacrament

When the church assembles, Word and Sacrament are to be at the very center of what the assembly does. Scripture readings and preaching, Baptism and Eucharist are not the only things that happen in worship, of course, and worship is not the only thing that churches do. But Word and Sacrament are the essential core of the assembly and so they are the foundation of all that the church says and does. The church may get a lot of things wrong, but it has nothing right unless it has Word and Sacrament. "The pure ministry of the Word and pure mode of celebrating the sacraments are," said Calvin, "sufficient pledge and guarantee that we may safely embrace as church any society in which both these marks exist. The principle extends to the point that we must not reject it so long as it retains them." Calvin was so committed to the constitutive centrality of these marks that he would embrace a church of the Word and Sacrament "even if it otherwise swarms with many faults."[10] So, before the church renews its programs or facilities, before the church revises its budget or structure, before the church reforms its evangelism or mission, it must ask the primary question: When the congregation assembles for worship on the Lord's Day and at other times during the week, is the word of God purely preached and heard, and are the sacraments purely celebrated according to Christ's institution?

Well, no, not really. Few ministers claim to preach the word purely, and even fewer imagine that their sermons are purely heard. People who listen to sermons every week know that there is nothing pure about preaching, and most are honest enough to admit that they are hard of hearing. Celebrating the sacraments in fidelity to Christ is even more problematic. More often than not, baptism and the Lord's Supper are relegated to occasional, peripheral elements of Presbyterian worship. Even allowing that our church life "swarms with many faults," we still seem to fail Calvin's Word and Sacrament purity test.

But Calvin was utterly realistic about the church. Since he had no interest in unattainable ideals, he recognized that "some fault may creep into the administration of either doctrine or sacraments, but this ought not to estrange us from communion with the church."[11] Apparently, perfect sermons, perfect hearing, and perfect sacraments are not required. What, then, is the point of all the talk about these essential marks of the church? How many faults may creep in before the markers become meaningless? Since Calvin was not indifferent to faulty sermons and sacraments, he tried to provide some theological guidance concerning all-too-evident faults and the truth of word and sacrament: "For not all the articles of true doctrine are of the same sort. Some are so necessary to know that they should be certain and unquestioned by all men as the proper principles of religion. Such are: God is one; Christ is God and the Son of God; our salvation rests in God's mercy; and the like. Among the churches there are other articles of doctrine disputed which still do not break the unity of faith."[12] This apparently casual list, followed by an impatient *et cetera*, does not help much, however. The marks may not have to be flawless, but shouldn't there be some standard of what is true and what is false, and some measure that determines whether we have departed from the truth?

At this point, we may become exasperated with Calvin. He seems to begin with clear criteria, only to add so many qualifications that we are left with little to go on. We may have our patience restored, however, when we realize that he was not interested in a firm list of "essential tenets" of the faith, nor was he erecting secure borders to separate who is right from who is wrong, who is in from who is out. His "marks" of the church function less as boundaries than as directional signs pointing to the core of ecclesial life. Any community claiming to be a *Christian church* must place proclamation of the gospel of Jesus Christ at the heart of its life, both through preaching and hearing the word and through faithful celebration of Baptism and the Lord's Supper. The question for any congregation or association of congregations is whether or not Word and Sacraments are found at the heart of common life. The centrality of congregational practice does not imply doctrinal indifference, of course. The word preached is Jesus Christ, the Word of God; the celebration of Baptism and Eucharist are sacraments of Jesus Christ, the icon of God. Thus, congregations gathered around Word and Sacrament are called to test their thinking, praying, and acting by the very marks that identify them as church and to test the marks themselves by the Truth of Jesus Christ.

Nevertheless, the basic question is whether Word and Sacrament identify the heart of the church's life. Proclamation in Word and Sacrament is not the only thing churches do, of course. Congregations (and denominations) engage in a wide variety of activities that go beyond preaching and teaching and celebration of the sacraments. But designating Word and Sacraments as marks of the true church means that other church activities must not bury Word and Sacrament, or push them to the periphery of church life, or place them in the service of other causes, whether justice or seeker-friendliness. Furthermore, the range of church activities must remain subject to authentication by Word and Sacrament, for these crucial realities are the embodiment of the gospel in the life of Christ's men and women. Word and Sacrament stand as the controlling core of ecclesial existence, the marks of a true church's life.

Do Presbyterian congregations pass Calvin's test? Sacramental minimalism in Reformed churches has pushed Baptism and the Lord's Supper to the periphery of congregational and denominational life. Reformed churches have tended not to be churches of the Word and Sacrament; too often they have been churches of the word alone. A church of the word alone is always in danger of becoming a church of *words* alone. Neglecting the sacraments while exalting words has often led to an obsession with verbal expression. Congregational worship is engulfed in a torrent of words, sweeping away silence, sight, gesture, and movement. Little wonder that James White calls Reformed worship "the most cerebral of the western traditions . . . prolix and verbose."[13] Similarly, Brian Gerrish notes that the wordiness of the Reformed tradition can result in "an arid intellectualism that turns the worshiping community into a class of glum schoolchildren."[14]

The danger in our focus on words goes deeper than problems of abstraction or boredom, however. Words are what we fight about, and words are what we fight with. Presbyterian and Reformed churches, so tied to words, are the churches that have divided and split more than Lutherans, or Episcopalians, or Catholics, or Orthodox. We imagine that our word-laden disputes and divisions are about the truth, of course. But we restrict truth to words—verbal formulations—in the conviction that words alone are adequate expressions of truth. Furthermore, our "truth words" are often turned into doctrinal weapons that obscure as well as exhibit the gospel. It may be that our history of schisms—always growing from disputes *about* words, always fought *with* words—is a result of our deficiency as a church, our failure to be a church of the Word and Sacrament.

Reformed sacramental practice, long neglected, continues to be marginalized in a tradition that exalts preaching and takes pride in theological precision. Massive, prominent pulpits loom over little tables graced with flowers and a Bible rather than bread and wine. Small bowls, often hidden, are usually bone dry. Too often, Reformed practice of Baptism is a mechanical ritual of infant identification. Even in its chummy American version, Baptism is little more than welcome into a gathering of people who are identified, rather arbitrarily, as a baby's new "family." The Lord's Supper, so recently a ritual of quarterly observance, may be on its way to becoming a monthly rite, but an arbitrary designation of the first Sunday of the month as "Communion Sunday" indicates its institutional rather than ecclesial function.

The need for a church of the Word and *Sacrament* is not based on vague or sentimental understandings of Baptism and Eucharist, however. Sacramental life is not a thick mist that blurs the sharp contours of the Word, nor do sacraments fully feed the life of faith, lessening need for the nourishing Word. Word and Sacrament are not contrasting aspects of church life: cognitive and affective, abstract and concrete, individual and communal, private and relational, head and heart. Renewal of sacramental life is not achieved at the expense of preaching. Warm communal affections, and emotional group ties are not the purpose of sacramental renewal.

The Presence of the Truth

Calvin placed Word and Sacrament together at the core of the church's true life because he knew that Jesus Christ is the center of the church's true life. Because Jesus Christ is the Truth, truth is to be found in Christ. Because Word and Sacrament are primary instances of Christ's presence in the church, they are marks of the church's fidelity to the Truth and to the truth about the Truth. Calvin took it as "a settled principle that the sacraments have the same office as the Word of God: to offer and set forth Christ to us, and in him the treasures of heavenly grace."[15] Calvin's view is remarkable in two ways. First, the purpose of the sacraments is the same as that of the word. Baptism and Eucharist are not expendable elements of worship, less important than Scripture and preaching, for they fulfill the same end. Presbyterians cannot imagine worship without Scripture and preaching. That we can imagine worship without the sacraments is a mark of our self-deprivation. Second, the purpose of both Word and Sacrament is to set forth Christ to us. In Word and Sacrament, Christ's presence becomes transparent and the benefits of Christ's presence become actual in the life of the assembly. Scripture and preaching are not for imparting information. Baptism and Eucharist are not for imparting feelings. Both Word and Sacraments are occasions for the real presence of Christ. The presence of the Truth gives Life to the community that now lives in God's new Way.

For Calvin, Word and Sacraments are efficacious: they give what they portray. Preaching God's word conveys Christ, continuing Christ's living presence. The sacraments re-present the person and work of Christ. "I say that Christ is the matter or (if you prefer) the substance of all the sacraments," says Calvin, "for in him they have all their firmness, and they do not promise anything apart from him."[16] Because Christ is the substance of the sacraments, the Lord's Supper and baptism are not merely occasions for the Christian community to celebrate its own life. The sacraments impart to the assembly the substance of its life in Christ.

If Word and Sacrament are at the heart of the church's true and faithful life, neglect of one leads inexorably to the deformation of the other. When either Word or Sacrament exists alone it soon becomes a parody of itself. Reformed Christians are aware of how easily the sacraments can become manipulative superstitions in churches where sacraments are exalted and preaching is minimalized. Reformed Christians may be less aware of how easily preaching and teaching can degenerate into institutional marketing or human potential promotion in churches that magnify the word while marginalizing Baptism and Eucharist. In the assembly, Word and Sacrament "offer and set forth Christ to us." In the assembly, Christ is the "matter and substance" of Scripture and preaching, Baptism and Eucharist. Word and Sacrament are each necessary to the other, and both together are essential modes of the presence of Christ among us.

Reformed confidence in the presence of Christ in Word and Sacrament lies behind the peculiar identification of preaching with the word of God. The Second Helvetic Confession claims boldly that "THE PREACHING OF THE WORD OF GOD IS THE WORD OF GOD." The confession goes on to assert that "when this Word of God is now preached in the church by preachers lawfully called, we believe that the very Word of God is proclaimed, and received by the faithful."[17]

As startling as this audacious claim appears, the virtual identification of preaching with the Word of God is not merely a sixteenth-century curiosity. The great twentieth-century theologian Karl Barth declared: "Proclamation is human language in and through which God Himself speaks, like a king through the mouth of his herald."[18] Even if we resist the claim that actual sermons we have preached or heard *are* the very Word of God, the theological association of the two underscores preaching's vital role in presenting Jesus Christ, the Word of God. Scripture, preaching, and teaching are not only means for hearing words *about* Christ, they are the way we hear *the* Word, the way Jesus Christ is set forth to us and is present with us.

A generation or two ago it was fashionable to engrave pulpits so that as preachers took their places they would encounter the words, "Sir, we would see Jesus" (John 12:21, KJV). Beneath the sentimentality of the practice lies the radical truth that the proclamation of the Word of God is the presence of Christ among us. Calvin's "Word of God purely preached and heard," then, is preaching of the gospel of Christ. "Pure" preaching is not infallible preaching, but preaching that has as its substance and goal the pure Word, Jesus Christ. The Word of God purely preached and heard is not aimed at inspirational encouragement, moral motivation, factional advocacy, or institutional advancement, but rather at the Word of the gospel. The proclamation of Christ may indeed inspire, motivate, advocate, or build up the church, but these can only flow from the Word, not become a substitute for the Word.

Proclamation is not limited to Sunday sermons. Proclamation is the church's witness to Jesus Christ, "offering and setting forth Christ to us" in creed and hymns, confession and praise, Scripture and intercessions, anthems and offerings. The worshiping assembly is the basic form of the church. Thus, Jesus Christ must be the matter and substance of the church's worship if the church is to preserve the truth, the gospel of the Truth. This does not mean that every part of worship must always make explicit reference to Christ, of course. But every part of worship must always be shaped by the grace of the Lord Jesus Christ, the love of God, and the communion of the Holy Spirit so that "true worshipers will worship *the Father* in *spirit* and *truth* "(John 4:23, 24).

An ancient Latin saying points up the centrality of the worshiping assembly to the preservation of the truth. *Lex orandi, lex credendi*—rule of praying, rule of believing—expresses the reality that the church's worship shapes its faith. How the church worships is the primary shaper of what worshipers believe. Worship that has Christ as its matter and substance forms a church that believes Christ and through him believes in one God, Father Son and Holy Spirit; trusts Christ and through him trusts the promises of God and the power of the Holy Spirit; is loyal to Christ, and through him is unwavering in love of God and life in the Spirit. Worship that has human wants and needs, aspirations and causes, as its matter and substance forms a church that believes in itself, trusts its programs, and is loyal to its institutions.

The worship of the assembly is so central to the preservation of the truth that the Latin saying can be reversed: The church's belief must shape its worship. Pastors, elders, musicians, and other worship planners must pay the closest theological attention to the order of worship and all of worship's elements in order to ensure that Word and Sacrament are at the heart of worship, and that all else flows from Word and Sacrament. The purpose of theologically shaped worship is not liturgical fussiness, or even liturgical renewal, but rather "setting forth Christ to us, and in him the treasures of heavenly grace." Thus, human needs and aspirations are not irrelevant. Freed from willful craving and consumption, they find their true fulfillment through the treasures of Christ's grace.

Ever Possible, Ever Present Evil

Even the best preaching is error-riddled, and celebrations of the sacraments are not free from disorder. We know from experience that worshiping assemblies—actual gatherings of believers in Pittsburgh and Pretoria, Edinburgh and Los Angeles—are far from ideal. We also know that denominations are flawed, ecumenical agencies are deficient, and communions of churches are imperfect. In all of its manifestations, the church is simply a gathering of persons who have been called and always are being called to new life by Christ. Our failings are apparent, but they are not the only reality. We are sinners and yet we are justified by the grace of Christ. We are sick and yet we are embraced in the love of God. We are lost and yet we are at home in the communion of the Holy Spirit. The novelist John Updike puts our situation well: "A company of believers is like a prisonful of criminals: their intimacy and solidarity are based on what about themselves they can least justify."[19] The assembly is not bound together by virtue or achievement, but by the reign of God inaugurated by Christ, by our repentance, and by our shared trust in our faithful Savior.

We are able to be utterly honest about the church's failings because we hear the call of God in Christ. The Nicene Creed affirms that the church—in the first instance the worshiping assembly that confesses the Creed—is "one, holy, catholic, and apostolic." Too often, we experience ourselves as divided, conformist, restrictive, and timid. Yet our all-too-apparent faults do not trump the Creed, for the church is the community where Christ's call is ever-present: Christ calls the church to be one, to embody a distinctive way of life, to include in its embrace all people, and to proclaim the truth of the gospel. The persistent presence of Christ's call is as real, and as constitutive of the church, as our feeble response.

The prayers of confession offered by Cardinal Ratzinger and Pope John Paul II raised the question: Does the *church* sin, or is sin confined to members of the church? The Reformed tradition has always been clear that the church is as liable to sin as are all of the church's members. Church members may depart from the truth, but so may the church itself. The Westminster Confession of Faith makes the point starkly: "The purest churches under heaven are subject both to mixture and error: and some have so degenerated as to become apparently no churches of Christ."[20] How, then, does the church preserve the truth? How can congregations, denominations, ecumenical councils, and communions of churches be expected to preserve the truth when all of them are "subject both to mixture and error"?

The church's responses to the truth may be ambiguous, yet Christ's call abides. The church may try to evade the truth, yet God's love endures. The church may fail to live the truth, yet the communion of the Holy Spirit perseveres. Because the church is the God-called, God-loved, God-shaped community, its ever possible and ever present errors do not bury the truth of the gospel. The church remains in the truth of the gospel in spite of its errors because the triune God remains faithful to the church.

The worshiping assembly is the fundamental form of the church, yet it is the form of the church that is most liable to error. Self-interest is a real and present danger in every congregation as church life is tailored to meet personal and organizational needs. Because congregations are always tempted to depart from the truth, it is essential that congregations unite in patterns of mutual responsibility and accountability. The Presbyterian Church (U.S.A.) and its presbyteries and synods provide relationships of shared answerability to the truth. Of course, a denomination is also prone to institutional self-interest that may marginalize the truth; thus, every denomination must be answerable to its congregations and to other denominations. Yet all denominations and their congregations exist in particular places, so they are susceptible to cultural myopia that fails to see the truth of the gospel with clarity. Churches in North America need the witness of churches in different cultures, just as those churches need North American churches and each other. Even this global span of ecclesial responsibility and accountability is not sufficient, however. At the beginning of the church's third millennium, we all need the witness to the truth given to us by all who have lived and died the faith before us. *The Book of Confessions* is a primary way that Presbyterians receive the wisdom of different eras in the church's life.

Every worshiping assembly, every denomination, the church in every place, and the church in every age is able to respond faithfully to the call to preserve the truth of the gospel only as they live out the creedal reality of "the communion of saints." What the French Confession says of individual Christians is true of congregations, denominations, places, and ages: "We believe that no one should withdraw from the church, satisfied to be solitary. The whole community must preserve and sustain the unity of the church, submitting to common instruction and to the yoke of Christ."[21]

Mother Church

Calvin uses a wonderfully suggestive image for the church: "Mother of All the Godly." He does not think the church is a woman, of course, but he does think that our relationship to the church is best likened to the relationship of children to a loving mother. "For there is no other way to enter into life," says Calvin, "unless this mother conceive us in her womb, give us birth, nourish us at her breast, and lastly, unless she keep us under her care and guidance. . . ."[22] Calvin is not romanticizing the church, but recognizing that, like a mother, the church births, nourishes, and nurtures our faith, teaching us the truth of the gospel and training us in truthful living.

In baptism, we are joined to Christ and incorporated into Christ's body. Helpless, unknowing infants are brought to the waters accompanied by the promises of the assembled congregation:

Do you, as members of the church of Jesus Christ,

promise to guide and nurture N. and N.

by word and deed,

with love and prayer,

encouraging them to know and follow Christ

and be faithful members of his church?

As we answer, "We do," we know that we answer on behalf of the holy catholic church, and that our promise is possible because others made and kept the promise to us. We also know that our answer's worth is dependent on our commitment to preserve the truth of the gospel for the church's children, nurturing them in the Word and nourishing them with the Sacraments.

Notes

1. Anne Tyler, *Saint Maybe* (New York: Alfred A. Knopf, 1991), p. 127.
2. Jürgen Moltmann, *The Church in the Power of the Spirit*, trans. Margaret Kohl (New York: Harper & Row, 1977), p. 289.
3. Ibid., pp. 294–295.
4. *Koinonia* is the Greek word for "communion" or "fellowship," and in Christianity it refers in particular to communion in the Holy Spirit.
5. *Perichoretic* describes the way in which the Persons of the Trinity—the Father Son and Holy Spirit—are fully and totally interrelated both in their unity and individuality.
6. *Proleptic*, as the word is used here, describes the way in which the church is a partial and imperfect manifestation of that which is yet to come in its fullness—the reign of God and the new humanity.
7. Wade Clark Roof, *Spiritual Marketplace* (Princeton, N.J.: Princeton University Press, 1999), p. 78.
8. Gordon Lathrop, *Holy People: A Liturgical Ecclesiology* (Minneapolis: Fortress Press, 1999), p. 5.
9. Calvin, *Institutes* 4.1.9, p. 1023.
10. Ibid., 4.1.12, p. 1025.
11. Ibid.
12. Ibid., 4.1.12, pp. 1025–1026.
13. James F. White, *Protestant Worship* (Louisville: Westminster John Knox Press, 1989), pp. 58–78.
14. B. A. Gerrish, *Grace and Gratitude* (Minneapolis: Fortress Press, 1993), p. 86.
15. Calvin, *Institutes* 4.14.17, p. 1292.
16. Ibid., 4.14.16, p. 1291.
17. Second Helvetic Confession, *The Book of Confessions*, 5.004.
18. Karl Barth, *Church Dogmatics*, vol. I, part 1, trans. G. T. Thomson (Edinburgh: T. & T. Clark, 1936), p. 57.
19. John Updike, *In the Beauty of the Lilies* (New York: Alfred A. Knopf, 1996), p. 416.
20. Westminster Confession of Faith, *BC*, 6.144.
21. *The French Confession of 1559*, trans. Ellen Babinsky and Joseph D. Small (Louisville: Office of Theology and Worship, Presbyterian Church (U.S.A.), 1998), Art. XXVI, p. 13.
22. Calvin, *Institutes* 4.1.4, p. 1016.

The True Word of God

> The adult members of society adverted to the Bible unreasonably often. What arcana! Why did they spread this scandalous document before our eyes? If they had read it, I thought, they would have hid it. They didn't recognize the vivid danger that we would, through repeated exposure, catch a case of its wild opposition to their world.
>
> —Annie Dillard, *An American Childhood*[1]

Why has a book about the preservation of the truth taken so long to deal with the authority of the Bible? Surely the church's preservation of the truth is dependent on its fidelity to Scripture! There is no doubt that Scripture is the polestar that keeps the church on course, guiding its faith and faithfulness. A quick sampling of the church's confessions discloses the church's commitment to Scripture and the integral relationship of the Bible to the truth:

> We judge, therefore, that from these Scriptures are to be derived true wisdom and godliness, the reformation and government of churches; as also instruction in all duties of piety; and, to be short, the confirmation of doctrines, and the rejection of all errors. (Second Helvetic Confession, *BC*, 5.003)

> The holy Scriptures of the Old and New Testaments are the Word of God, the only rule of faith and obedience. (Westminster Larger Catechism, *BC*, 7.113)

> Try the spirits whether they are of God! Prove also the words of the Confessional Synod of the German Evangelical Church to see whether they agree with Holy Scripture and with the Confessions of the Fathers. If you find that we are

speaking contrary to Scripture, then do not listen to us! But if you find that we are taking our stand upon Scripture, then let no fear or temptation keep you from treading with us the path of faith and obedience to the Word of God. (Theological Declaration of Barmen, *BC*, 8.04)

The Scriptures are not a witness among others, but the witness without parallel. The church has received the books of the Old and New Testaments as prophetic and apostolic testimony in which it hears the word of God and by which its faith and obedience are nourished and regulated. (Confession of 1967, *BC*, 9.27)

While the confessions are clear about the centrality of Scripture, they are less interested in a doctrine of scriptural inspiration and authority than in the Bible's indispensable role in shaping the faith and life of the church and its members. The confessions assert boldly that Scripture gives wisdom and godliness, reforms the church, provides theological and ethical standards, tests the spirits of the age, and nourishes faith and obedience. The confessions are more concerned about the dynamic role of the Bible in the church, what Scripture *does*, than theories about the Bible's status.

Our confessional sampling leaves us with a puzzle, however. If Scripture is essential to the church's faith and life, why do we hear so many laments over biblical illiteracy and "the strange silence of the Bible in the church"? Why do too many church members know too little about the book they are told is central to an understanding of Christian faith, vital to the living of Christian discipleship? How can Christians neglect the writings that show the truth about faith and life? How can the church preserve the truth of the gospel if the Bible is not at the center of its life?

Problems, Problems, Problems

Presbyterians are no longer restricted to leather-bound, gilt-edged, tissue paper editions of the Authorized, "King James" Version of the Bible. Bibles are available in a wide variety of shapes and bindings, in all price ranges, and in a bewildering array of translations and paraphrases. Special study editions are produced for every demographic group, and gift editions are created for every occasion. Publishers go to the considerable trouble and expense of translation, enhancements, and production because Bibles sell. And yet, in spite of the unprecedented availability of the Bible, many people open the Scriptures only to find themselves on a magical mystery tour through obscure history, intricate arguments, ancient laws, baffling symbols, and incredible miracles. Because too much of the Bible seems too hard to understand, Bible reading becomes sporadic. The best intentions become bogged down midway through Leviticus; even people who read the Bible regularly confine themselves to familiar, intelligible passages.

The problem of understandability is compounded by uncertainty about the relevance of ancient writings to the complexities of modern life. People who are convinced *that* the Bible speaks to the contemporary situation, may be uncertain *how* the Scriptures are relevant. Can we draw lines between Old Testament history and current conflicts in the Middle East? Do healing stories have anything to say about today's health care crisis? What does squabbling in the church at Corinth have to do with divisions in the PC(USA)? Even clear biblical injunctions such as "You shall not kill" do not apply unambiguously to difficult moral issues such as capital punishment and euthanasia.

Problems of understandability and relevance are deepened by confusion about the scope of biblical authority. Even if we understand fully the Old Testament book of Habakkuk, determine that it is relevant to our time, and identify a passage that expresses a clear position on an important contemporary issue, what weight does it carry in our decision-making? Does the Bible override all other considerations and overrule all other authorities? Once we have determined "what the Bible says," is the matter closed?

As real as these problems are, questions of understandability, relevance, and authority are not the most unsettling problem of the Bible in the church. Before people deal with theoretical matters of biblical authority and interpretation, they must get over the first hurdle: the way they encounter the Bible in the church, especially in worship. The strange silence of the Bible begins with the way Scripture is used in the church's worship, the weekly way people come into contact with the Old and New Testaments.

The Word of the Lord, Thanks Be to God!

Several years ago, Presbyterian Research Services conducted a national survey that asked church members about their actual use of the Bible. The survey confirmed what we already know: Most Presbyterians receive all the Bible they will get during the week through their ears, in church, on Sunday morning. A majority of Presbyterians do not read the Bible regularly, study the Bible, or reflect devotionally on the Bible. Their near-exclusive contact with the Scriptures is what they hear read during worship. Even in the most responsible congregations, Bible studies are for the few. In homes, offices, factories, and schools, Bibles are neglected. The Scriptures are not *read*, they are *heard* in the context of weekly worship.

Is this such a bad thing? After all, worship is the Bible's natural home. Before it finds its way to the church school, private study, personal devotions, group meetings, or scholarly examination, the Bible lives in the congregation's worship. Detached from gratitude and praise of God, Scripture can be reduced to a textbook, an instruction manual, or a collection of self-help bromides. Receiving the Bible through our ears in worship only makes us like most Christians throughout history as well as in many parts of the world today. Historically, most Christians have encountered this written word of God, not by reading, but by hearing.

Our problem is not that we encounter the Bible in worship. Our difficulty grows from the *way* we encounter the Bible in worship. The Bible is not absent from worship, of course, for every Sunday service includes one or more Scripture readings. Yet these readings pop up as disconnected snippets, brief fragments abstracted from a discernible whole. What can it mean for most church members, unfamiliar with the Scriptures, to hear the minister intone, "From the eleventh chapter of Ezekiel, beginning with the second verse, hear the word of God"? The disconcerting reality is that many of those who receive the Bible through their ears on Sunday morning are not prepared to hear anything at all! In worship, the reading of the Bible is too often met with glazed eyes and wandering minds.

Most worshipers are not equipped to listen, making it difficult to hear anything, much less the word of God. Scripture readings skip around the Bible from testament to testament, book to book, with no consistent, enduring presentation of anything. The lack of integrity in Sunday Scripture readings may be connected to a perception, shared by ministers and members alike, that the readings are mere preludes to preaching. Ministers often read texts as the preliminary ground of their sermons, not as independently powerful proclamations of God's Way among us. Members may think they do not have to pay attention to Bible readings because they are merely a preface to the minister's sermon.

The situation is only marginally better for the minority of members who find their way into the church's Bible studies. All too often, Bible study is either a strangely impersonal historical examination of ancient writings, or an oddly over-personal search for spiritual fulfillment, or a peculiar quest for successful living guidelines. Bible study that is an archaeological excavation of old texts is not likely to be heard as a witness to God's active presence among us now. Bible study that is a variation on self-help programs is not likely to be heard as a witness to God's abiding presence with the whole creation and its peoples.

None of this is true of every Presbyterian church member, of course. Yet it is true enough of enough Presbyterians to present a major impediment to hearing the word of God, moving the Scriptures to the edges of congregational and personal discipleship.

The situation is only marginally different for Presbyterian ministers. Many, perhaps most ministers spend their time with the Bible in lectionary -ordered weekly snippets that serve as instruments for the preparation of sermons. The Scriptures are narrowed to small passages, and then further narrowed in the search for a preachable moment. Ministers also spend time with Scripture in preparation for teaching the Bible to church groups, but here the emphasis is on what to teach about the Bible, not on the Bible as the word of God for the minister. The tragedy of many ministers is that they do not read the Scriptures regularly, study them carefully, or reflect on them devotionally, except as raw material for frequent preaching and occasional teaching. The Bible becomes the means to an end rather than a source of life.

Throughout the church, disciplined, extensive, attentive reading of Scripture is uncommon; disciplined, sustained, in-depth study of the Bible is infrequent; disciplined, imaginative, obedient spiritual exposure to the Scriptures is rare.

Biblical Data

Ironically, the lectionary—the regular table of readings for each Lord's Day—bears some responsibility for neglect of the Bible. For all of its many advantages, and for all its contributions to more biblical preaching, the lectionary tends to confirm a distortion of the Bible that grows from its artificial division into chapters and verses. We are so used to chapters and verses that we do not realize that these partitions are strange intrusions into the Scriptures. The integrity of varied biblical writings—narratives, letters, poems, prophesies—is jeopardized as they are divided and subdivided into numbered paragraphs, sentences, and phrases. Chapters and verses are a convenience, devised by rabbis, medieval monks, and, finally, printers, enabling us to locate ourselves within a text. But it is a convenience that we would not think of asking from a novel, a biography, or a letter from a friend.

Our problem is that versification of the Bible can lead to disastrous distortions. We are all heirs to the assumption that there is an "objective" understanding of the world that can be known through the "scientific method" for ordering and understanding reality. Thus, we tend to view lectionary-ordered passages with their chapters and verses as free-standing bits of data that can be gathered as evidence in the demonstration of a "truth." The marvelous variety of diverse biblical writings is flattened out as a verse from Mark's Gospel is joined to two verses from Jeremiah and one more from Romans and these together become facts that are used to argue a point or demonstrate a theological certainty. We think nothing of burrowing into the cohesive narrative of John's Gospel, extracting the verse, "You shall know the truth and the truth shall make you free," and treating the phrase as a timeless axiom, independent of its place in John's story of Jesus the Christ. Or we jump into Paul's letter to the Christian congregations in Rome and hold up the phrase, "Let every person be subject to the governing authorities," as if it were the divine truth about issues of church and state.

Several years ago I read a good mystery novel, *Smilla's Sense of Snow*, by the Danish writer Peter Høeg. Like most novels, the book is divided into chapters, but that is merely a device to signal a change in scene. Like all novels, the chapters are not divided into verses. Early in the narrative Smilla says, "I feel the same way about solitude as some people feel about the blessings of the church. It's the light of grace for me."[2] That is an interesting thought, but apart from the whole story its meaning is obscure. Who is Smilla? Where does the story take place? What is happening? Because I enjoyed *Smilla's Sense of Snow* I might want to tell friends about the novel, saying a bit about its plot and characters, but I would not analyze these two sentences apart from the whole.

If my friends had read the novel, we might have an interesting conversation about solitude and grace within the structure of the book, but if they knew little or nothing about *Smilla's Sense of Snow*, my talk about the book's treatment of solitude and grace would have an oddly detached quality. It would seem particularly odd if I coupled Høeg's two sentences with a scene from John Updike's novel *Roger's Version*:

"Where on earth are you going?" I asked her.

"Obviously," she said, "to church."

"Why would you do a ridiculous thing like that?"

"Oh —" She appraised me with her pale green eyes. Whatever emotions had washed through her had left an amused glint, a hint or seed. In her gorgeous rounded woman's voice she pronounced smilingly, "To annoy you."[3]

Odder still would be a claim that the two excerpts together demonstrated a universal truth about the church, or grace, or contemporary culture.

We are all aware of the danger. We recognize the impropriety of "taking out of context" and "proof-texting." Yet if we receive the Bible in brief, lectionary ordered, independent passages each a few verses in length, the likelihood increases that the Bible will be seen as a collection of disembodied "truths" that can be arranged to argue a case and demonstrate a conclusion. For the less contentious among us, brief bits of Scripture may appear more like mottos, inspirational quotes suitable for framing. Too often, the Bible is employed as if its sentences were logical axioms or gems from Bartlett's *Familiar Quotations*. In either case, we have reduced the Scriptures to isolated bits of data.

Have I stated the matter too starkly? Is the situation better than my bleak analysis? Perhaps. But even if I have exaggerated (and I do not think I have), few would claim that the whole Bible lives at the church's center, providing the common ground of our faith and life, the shared source for the resolution of our conflicts. The problem does not lie in what we believe about the Bible, but rather in the fragmented ways the Bible functions in the ongoing life of the worshiping assembly and other gatherings of the church.

Corrective Lenses

A hint about the way Scripture might function in the life of the church is found in one of John Calvin's marvelously suggestive images. Calvin notes that as people grow older, their eyesight may become a bit dim, their vision a bit fuzzy. It began earlier for me. When I was in my twenties I began to notice that I could not read distant road signs. I needed eyeglasses. When I was in my forties I had to hold books farther and farther away from my eyes. I needed bifocals. In order to see the world clearly, in order to read easily, I had to have corrective lenses.

Calvin says that our perception of God and God's Way in the world suffers a similar defect. We do not perceive God clearly. When we look at the world around us we do not see God's presence in sharp focus, if we see it at all. Our vision of God and God's Way is dim, fuzzy, and distorted. Scripture, says Calvin, is like a pair of spectacles, the corrective lenses that enable us to see God clearly and to perceive God's Way plainly. Without the corrective lenses of Scripture, we are nearsighted or farsighted or both. But with the spectacles of the Bible we can discern who God is, who we are, how God cares for us, and how we can live together in God's presence, knowing what direction to move in, and what to do along the way.[4]

Calvin's image is suggestive, not only as a whole, but also in the details. My eyeglasses only work as an integrated instrument. One lens will not correct my vision, and within each lens it takes two prescriptions working together to enable me to see everything clearly. Moreover, the purpose of my glasses is to let me see the world, not to provide an object for my examination. I spend little time focusing my attention on my glasses. I use my glasses to see everything else. If I were to focus on the lenses, the temples, the little nose pads, and the bridge, I would miss the purpose of the glasses themselves.

I have to understand what my glasses are for and how they work. I must care for them properly and use them regularly. So, too, with the Scriptures. We must know what they are and what they are for—God's good gift to us, allowing us to see clearly God's gracious and judging presence among us. We must not misuse Scripture by breaking it apart into little bits. We must use the Bible consistently as cohesive narratives that enable us to see the presence of God in our midst.

The Bible is not the exclusive object of our examination, as if we were studying Homer's *Odyssey* or reading an account of Lewis and Clark's expedition. Our purpose in reading or hearing Scripture is to see God more plainly, to perceive ourselves more honestly, to view the world more fully, to pay closer attention to the paths laid out in front of us. Who of us does not want that accurate vision of the truth about God and ourselves? I do not go through a single day without my glasses. What would our church be like if it did not go through a week without the clear perception made possible through the Scriptures?

Frederick Buechner, a novelist and Presbyterian minister, provides an intriguing variation on Calvin's image of the Bible as our corrective lenses. "If you look *at* a window," says Buechner, "you see fly specks, dust, the crack where Junior's Frisbie hit it. If you look *through* a window, you see the world beyond. Something like this is the difference between those who see the Bible as a Holy Bore and those who see it as the Word of God which speaks out of the depths of an almost unimaginable past into the depths of ourselves."[5]

Buechner's window is like Calvin's eyeglasses: both are meant to be looked through, not examined for their own sake. Buechner's window adds something important to Calvin's glasses, however. A window is something we can look through together. My glasses are for me alone; I am the only one who looks through them. But we can all gather around a window, a big window that lets us look out together on the world. As we look through the window together we can tell each other what we see. Some of us may notice things that others do not. Some may be attentive to features of the landscape while others focus on people. Some may take in the whole vista, others may concentrate on one part of the view. But we can talk to each other, drawing one another's attention to the things we see. Standing at the window together, talking with one another, we can discover features of the world we would not have seen by ourselves.

The Bible provides us with a truthful view of who God is, who we are, what God has to do with us, and how we could live together. The Bible provides *us* with that view, all of us together. The Bible is not meant to be read alone or to be listened to in isolation from other hearers. St. Augustine, the early church bishop and theologian, relates an amusing anecdote that illustrates Scripture's communal nature. One day, as Augustine and his companions walked down a hallway in the church in Milan, they saw the oddest sight: Bishop Ambrose was reading the Bible to himself, silently. There is nothing odd to us about a person reading silently; that is how we read the Bible most of the time. But that is not how people used to read, so that the sight of Ambrose reading silently to himself was so unusual that Augustine tried to explain it. Perhaps Ambrose was angry with the young men . . . perhaps he was in a great hurry . . . perhaps he had a sore throat. Augustine could not understand individual, silent reading of the Scriptures, but he thought so much of Ambrose that he concluded, "Whatever his motive was in so doing, it was doubtless, in such a man, a good one."[6]

In a time before the ready availability of printed copies of the Bible, the Scriptures were read aloud, in a gathered community of Christians. The leader, often the bishop or a priest, but sometimes a lay teacher, read aloud, perhaps offering some interpretive comments. Persons in the gathered community were free to interrupt the reading with questions, observations, or insights. The Bible was a "group activity," a gathering of the community around the "window" to talk about what they saw. Everything is different now, so that the contemporary ideal— even if we seldom meet it—is for individuals to read, study, and contemplate the Scriptures by themselves. When the Bible is read aloud, in the assembly's worship, hearers are expected to listen passively, no matter how puzzled or inspired they may be.

Our question, then, is how we can rescue the Scriptures from being ignored at worst, and being imprisoned within the lone individual at best. How can the Bible become the *church's* book again, so that it can be voiced and heard as an announcement of the Word of God? How can Scripture become the *church's* book again, so that it can be the corrective lenses we need to see the truth about God and ourselves?

Believing Is Seeing

As we become better able to hear the Bible, Scripture is better able to serve as the corrective lenses (or the window) enabling us to see the truth about God's Way in our midst. Hearing and seeing, sound and scene, combine to move us beyond narrow understandings of the Bible as information or propositions. Scripture does impart information about Israel, Jesus of Nazareth, and the early church, but historical facts are in the service of a wider vision. Scripture also contains propositions, but rational discourse is placed within a broader perspective. What do we hear and see in and through Scripture?

What we see most immediately is a world, but it soon becomes clear that it is not simply the tangible world of empirical observation. The Scriptures do not speak only in descriptive language about a world that is past, or in didactic language about a world that is available for manipulation. Instead, Scripture projects a new world before us, a world of transformed human relationships under the coming reign of God, a place where we could live.

The new world projected before us by the biblical texts is filled with the presence of God. This means more than that the texts speak about God. God is present in the world of the Scriptures as the gravitational field that grounds all of the narratives, prophecies, laws, wisdom, hymns, and letters. The God of Scripture's new world is not a generic deity, but the God who is shown to us and abides with us in Jesus Christ, who remains with us in the power of the Holy Spirit. The world of biblical texts is a world structured in relation to God, constituted in relation to Christ, and sustained in relation to the Spirit, all in ways that disclose new possibilities for human living.

The world of the Bible is not the world we live in. It is not the sphere of autonomous attainment, the new world order of marketplace economies, or the arena of American cultural hegemony. The world of the Scriptures is God-shaped, a *new* world in which we *could* dwell.

The Bible is not simply a witness to the revelation of God that occurred long ago and far away. Scripture itself is revelation, but what is revealed is not knowledge, or propositional statements, or timeless verities. Scripture reveals God-shaped possibilities for new life in a God-shaped new world. What is revealed is not primarily *knowledge about* such a world, but rather the *discernment* of this world as a place where we could dwell.

Biblical writings are not straightforward descriptions of familiar realities, but the manifestation of unfamiliar possibilities. What Scripture shows us is a *proposed* world that emerges from the ruins of everyday experience and taken-for-granted reality. To interpret biblical texts, then, is to appropriate their truth for ourselves. The Bible invites us to understand ourselves in terms of the proposed world, to orient ourselves to that world, to move toward life in that world. The world we see through the lenses of Scripture is not just any world and not merely my world, but a redeemed world lived within the reign of God. God's world is not a historical restoration of past hopes, but the present possibility of a future that lies in front of us. The Jesus who calls us into this new world is not a historical reconstruction, but the risen and present Christ. The Holy Spirit who infuses this new world is not a private comfort, but the reconciling presence of God to create genuine human community.

Suspicious Eyes

The Scriptures are the corrective lenses that enable us to see the truth of who God is, who we are, what God has to do with us, and how we could live together. The Bible is our window on that world. Yet problems of understandability, relevance, and authority are not easily dismissed. Do the Scriptures give glimpses of a lovely vision that eludes everyone but the experts? Is the Bible's contemporary significance really clear? Does the authority of Scripture trump all other authorities?

When we take the Bible seriously we may find ourselves suspended between two poles: the pole of naive acceptance and the pole of disquieting suspicion. On the one hand, Scripture is a source of insight and inspiration. On the other hand, the Bible comes under question because modern standards of science, history, and justice seem to undermine its trustworthiness. However, taking the Bible seriously means neither burying suspicions nor discarding Scripture. Instead, we can work through naive acceptance and sophisticated skepticism in a faithful attempt to gain new vision.

All too often the church tries to keep doubts at bay by calling for simple trust in the Scriptural witness. This is misguided, not only because it fails to protect us from the onslaught of suspicion, but because it also prevents us from seeing clearly the full vision that the

Scriptures project before us. However, refusing to remain within the false security of naive reception does not mean that we must dwell in the wasteland of suspicion. Some people dismiss Scripture as nothing more than prescientific mythology, while others reject the Bible as a denigration of women or a tool of the powerful. This "modern" attitude remains barren. It not only denies the very openness modernity champions, but it blinds us to the new vision the Scriptures project.

Clear sight comes when we subject innocent faith and uncritical reception to the rigors of suspicion . . . and then suspect our own suspicion! We cannot avoid questions about the Bible that are part of contemporary culture. Nor should we. Suspicions about biblical testimony enable us to see beyond the surface so that we can view the depth of God's gracious Way in the world. New vision does not result automatically from our suspicion, of course. The suspicions that arise from our modernity must be subjected to the Bible's suspicion of our own preconceptions. Do we doubt the assumptions and standards of ancient Israel or the first-century church because we have absolutized the assumptions and standards of twenty-first-century North America? There is a peculiar arrogance in asserting that our way of perceiving reality is *the* way of seeing. Questioning the Bible is necessary if we are to move beyond elementary understanding. Yet this will only mire us in our culture's version of "the way things are" unless we employ a second suspicion, a suspicion with respect to ourselves. This does not mean abandoning our own times in an uncritical return to the past. It does mean subjecting our times to courageous critique so that we can see a new vision of our times through the lenses of Scripture.

Seeing the Truth

Pages of talk *about* the Bible cannot produce a full vision of the truth or help the church to preserve the truth. Knowing and preserving the truth takes new ways of reading the Bible. John Burgess suggests four new ways (actually four very old ways) to read Scripture so that we can really hear and truly see. "Over the centuries," says Burgess, "four disciplines in particular have helped Christians to nurture such a piety [of the Word]: reading Scripture aloud, reading Scripture in community, reading Scripture in context, and memorizing Scripture."[7]

Reading Scripture aloud, even when one is reading alone, engages senses of sound and feeling as well as sight. Our eyes see printed words, we give voice to sight through breath and tongue, and our ears receive the words anew. Intonation becomes interpretation as we read to ourselves the way we read to children and grandchildren. Thus the sounds of the Scriptures help us to see into the words, and through the words, to see with new vision into the truth about God and ourselves.

Yet Scripture is meant to be read with others, in community. As we read aloud to one another we can pause to talk about what we hear and see, questioning, exploring, and discovering. In community we are not limited by our own perception; we are enriched by the perception of others. Community reading of Scripture is face-to-face and voice-to-voice, but reading together should also be open to the voices of Christians in our denomination and in other situations, places, and times. Just as individual sight is insufficient, the vision of a small community is limited. We need the insights of "the communion of saints" in order to perceive the whole truth about God and ourselves.

Bible reading should respect the integrity of the Scriptures. The Bible is a collection of writings, each of which speaks in its own voice to provide a particular angle of vision on God's Way in the world. Reading through Mark's Gospel, the narratives of 1 and 2 Samuel, Paul's letter to the Galatians, or any "book" of the Bible, gives full voice to what each one sees. Reading and hearing in large, continuous, complete blocks enables us to see the whole landscape rather than small fragments of the picture.

Finally, Scripture should be remembered. Word-for-word memorization of some portions of Scripture may be helpful. Psalm 23; John 1:1–18; Romans 8:31–39, and other texts essential to Christian faith and life can be recalled at crucial moments in order to renew the vision of God's Way in the world. Other portions of Scripture can be remembered in their purpose and movement so that they remain accessible. Remembering the narrative of Israel's exodus from slavery to freedom, Jesus' parables, and Paul's wrestling with Israel's election in Romans 9—11 can evoke the broad picture of God's presence.

These four disciplines—practices that require intention and effort—have counterparts in the church's public worship. How can congregations reshape worship so that Scripture is read skillfully, enabling the worshipers to hear and see? In what ways can the Scriptures engage the whole congregation in active listening and imaginative vision? How can Scripture readings be planned and introduced so that the sweep of particular biblical witnesses is followed week after week? Can the presence of the Bible in worship encourage the memory that gives birth to hope? These are not easy questions to answer, and there is no formula that will fit every congregation. But answers must be sought so that the truth may be heard, seen, and lived. Thus is the truth preserved.

Notes

1. Annie Dillard, *An American Childhood* (New York: Harper & Row, Quality Paperback, 1990), p. 134.
2. Peter Høeg, *Smilla's Sense of Snow* (New York: Dell, 1993), p. 11.
3. John Updike, *Roger's Version* (New York: Alfred A. Knopf, 1986), p. 329.
4. See Calvin, *Institutes* 1.6.1 (p. 70) and 1.14.1 (p. 160).
5. Frederick Buechner, *Wishful Thinking: A Theological ABC* (New York: Harper & Row, 1973), p. 12.
6. Augustine, *Confessions*, 3.3, trans. and ed. Albert C. Outler (Philadelphia: Westminster Press, 1955), p. 116.
7. John Burgess, *Why Scripture Matters* (Louisville: Westminster John Knox Press, 1998), p. 59. See the chapter "A Piety of the Word," pp. 58–78.

Tradition

> We live everything as it comes, without warning, like an
> actor going on cold. And what can life be worth if the first
> rehearsal for life is life itself? That is why life is always a
> sketch. No, "sketch" is not quite the word, because a sketch
> is an outline of something, the groundwork for a picture,
> whereas the sketch of our life is a sketch for nothing, an
> outline with no picture.
>
> —Milan Kundera, *The Unbearable Lightness of Being*[1]

Sola gratia. Sola fide. Sola scriptura. "Grace alone, faith alone, scripture alone" are the three great maxims of the sixteenth-century Reformation. "Grace alone" points us toward the reality of God's initiative rather than to human striving. "Faith alone" points us toward gratitude for God's grace rather than to human achievement. "Scripture alone" points us toward God's revelation rather than to human deduction. All three are meant as positive proclamations, but they have often been understood tendentiously, as sharp critiques of the Catholic Church. This has been especially true of s*ola scriptura*, which is sometimes understood to mean that Protestants look exclusively to Scripture while Catholics exalt tradition, placing it on an equal footing with Scripture. Not only is this a caricature of the Catholic understanding of Scripture and tradition, it misses the irony that s*ola scriptura* is itself part of the Protestant tradition! Nevertheless, freed from overtones of anti-Catholic polemic, it can be said that Protestants generally, and Reformed Protestants in particular, believe that all tradition is contingent and must be accountable to Scripture.

Ad fontes was the slogan of Renaissance humanism: back to the sources. *Ad fontes* gave birth to *sola scriptura*. The Scriptures are the source of the church's knowledge of the grace of the Lord Jesus Christ, the love of God, and the communion of the Holy Spirit, and so it is to Scripture that the church must always return. The Bible is far more than a relic of the past, a progression of museum exhibits that lets us look at life long ago and far away. A sixteenth-century confession from Switzerland expresses the Reformation's core teaching about Scripture, the church, and Christ: "The holy Christian Church, whose only head is Christ, is born of the Word of God, abides in the same, and listens not to the voice of a stranger."[2] The community of faith is the creation of the Word of God, not an institution of human construction. The community of faith hears the Word of God in the words of Scripture and does not heed competing voices from the world. This bedrock conviction is more than a sixteenth-century curiosity, for it continues to guide the church. The twentieth-century Theological Declaration of Barmen, written in the face of the Nazi threat to the integrity of the gospel, puts the issue starkly:

> Jesus Christ, as he is attested for us in Holy Scripture, is the one Word of God which we have to hear and which we have to trust and obey in life and in death.

> We reject the false doctrine, as though the church could and would have to acknowledge as a source of its proclamation, apart from and besides this one Word of God, still other events and powers, figures and truths, as God's revelation.[3]

Sola scriptura, Not Scripture in Isolation

The Bible is at the center of the church's faithful witness, but the community of faith is not formed merely by the simple reading of Scripture. If the Bible were self-sufficient there would be no need for sermons following the reading of Scripture, or for Bible commentaries and other aids to sermon preparation. There would be no need in the church for Bible studies, and books about the Bible would be superfluous. Sermons, commentaries, study groups, and books are all necessary, however, because the meaning of the Scriptures is not always self-evident. The Bible does not stand alone, either in worship or in the broader life of the church. A central purpose of theology— including this book—is to assist the church in its faithful reading of Scripture. John Calvin wrote his comprehensive theological work, the *Institutes of the Christian Religion*, in order to provide a guide to the reading of Scripture: "Although Holy Scripture contains a perfect doctrine, . . . yet a person who has not much practice in it has good reason for some guidance and direction, to know what he ought to look for in it, in order not to wander hither and thither. . . ."[4] Scripture is never isolated, for it is always accompanied by study, discussion, interpretation, preaching, commentary, and theological writing. Within the community of faith, persons interpret Scripture in order to help each other determine what is faithful to the Word of God and what is the voice of a stranger.

Reformed churches have always expressed their understanding of Scripture's message by composing confessions of faith as public testimony to the scriptural truth of the gospel. Calvin had a high view of the unity of the church, acknowledging that "the church universal is a multitude gathered from all nations; . . . [it] agrees on the one truth of divine doctrine, and is bound by the bond of the same religion." Yet he also recognized that the church "is divided and dispersed in separate places. . . . Under it are thus included individual churches, disposed in towns and villages according to human need, so that each rightly has the name and authority of the church."[5] The dispersion of the church is geographical, temporal, and cultural. "Human need" leads churches in different times and places to express Christian conviction in their own contexts, without fracturing unity in the faith.

The necessity and freedom to express the faith contextually has led Reformed churches to be confession-making churches. In different times and various circumstances, churches have given present testimony to their faith and action. In the sixteenth century alone, Reformed churches produced more than sixty confessions of faith. The World Alliance of Reformed Churches has published a representative collection of more than twenty-five Reformed confessions from the twentieth century. This great variety of Reformed confessions is not an accident of history and geography. Reformed emphasis on the sovereignty of God and the primacy of Scripture leads to an acute awareness of the dangers of idolatry, including the idolatry of creeds and confessions. Thus, Reformed churches rarely identify a particular confession of faith as the only authoritative expression of Christian faith. That is one reason why the Presbyterian Church (U.S.A.)'s confessional standard is a *Book of Confessions*, a collection of eleven creeds, confessions, and catechisms spanning nearly eighteen centuries.

The Reformed *tradition* understands the formulation of confessions to be part of the mandate of proclamation entrusted to the church. Thus, churches belonging to the Reformed family have been inclined to state their deepest convictions in every place and time. All of this is stated succinctly in the Confession of 1967. The Preface begins with the conviction that "The church confesses its faith when it bears a present witness to God's grace in Jesus Christ." The need for *present* witness has always been a feature of the church's life, for "in every age, the church has expressed its witness in words and deeds as the need of the time required. . . . No one type of confession is exclusively valid, no one statement is irreformable."[6]

Confessions of faith, so important to the spread of the Reformation and so central to the church's continuing proclamation of the gospel, are not set above, or even on a par with, Scripture. John Knox's Preface to the Scots Confession expresses an understanding of the relationship between Scripture and confessions of faith that is as instructive for the contemporary church as it was in 1560: ". . . if any man will note in our Confession any chapter or sentence contrary to God's Holy Word, that it would please him of his gentleness and for Christian charity's sake to inform us of it in writing; and we, upon our honour, do promise him that by God's grace we shall give him satisfaction from the mouth of God, that is, from Holy Scripture, or else we shall alter whatever he can prove to be wrong."[7] Every articulation of Christian faith is always subject to the reforming power of the Bible.

Sola scriptura does not mean "Scripture alone to the exclusion of everything else." It does mean that everything else, from creeds and confessions to early and modern theology must be measured by the standard of the Scriptures. A Latin theological formulation captures this understanding of Scripture's place in the church's continuing theological life: *norma normans sed non normata*—"the norm that norms but is not normed." Scripture is the standard for all other authorities and is not itself subject to any other authority. The Latin phrase is a shorthand expression of the Bible's primacy, but it does not isolate Scripture by imagining that the Bible is the *only* authority for the church's faith and life. Other authorities of greater and lesser importance have a claim on us, even though no authority is independent of Scripture's assessment. The French Confession of 1559 puts the matter nicely: "We acknowledge these books [of Scripture] to be canonical, the most certain rule of our faith. . . . The Spirit leads us to distinguish the books of Scripture from other ecclesiastical books that may be useful, but upon which no article of faith can be based."[8] Clearly, Scripture is preeminent, but "other ecclesiastical books" are useful, including the old "books" of history, tradition, and the witness of the communion of saints, as well as newer books of commentary and study, theology and the Christian life.

The Tradition of Scripture

Scripture and tradition are inextricably bound. This is nowhere more evident than in our relationship to Scripture itself. Most Christians do not read the Old Testament in Hebrew and the New Testament in Greek. In worship and in study we encounter the Bible in an English translation, and the translations we use are the products of various translation traditions. Most of the Scripture citations in this book come from the New Revised Standard Version (NRSV), published in 1989 as "an authorized revision of the Revised Standard Version, published in 1952, which was a revision of the American Standard Version, published in 1901, which, in turn, embodied earlier revisions of the King James Version, published in 1611." The NRSV is a translation "in the tradition of the King James Bible," a tradition that embraces a commitment to be "as literal as possible."[9]

Other translation traditions are evident in the many English versions that have appeared in recent decades. The popular *Good News Bible: Today's English Version* (TEV) is committed to expressing Scripture's "meaning in a manner and form easily understood by the readers."[10] Eugene Peterson's *The Message* is a paraphrase rather than a translation, and so continues in the tradition of J. B. Phillips and Charles Williams: "The goal is not to render a word-for-word conversion of Greek into English, but rather to convert the tone, the rhythm, the events, the ideas, into the way we actually think and speak."[11] Different translation traditions can lead to very different renditions of the same biblical text. A typical example is 2 Corinthians 5:18–19:

> All this is from God, who reconciled us to himself through Christ, and has given us the ministry of reconciliation; that is, in Christ God was reconciling the world to himself, not counting their trespasses against them, and entrusting the message of reconciliation to us. (NRSV)

> All this is done by God, who through Christ changed us from enemies into his friends and gave us the task of making others his friends also. Our message is that God was making all mankind his friends through Christ. God did not keep an account of their sins, and he has given us the message which tells how he makes them his friends. (TEV)

> All this comes from the God who settled the relationship between us and him, and then called us to settle our

relationships with each other. God put the world square with himself through the Messiah, giving the world a fresh start by offering the forgiveness of sins. God has given us the task of telling everyone what he is doing. (*The Message*)

It is useful to know the tradition that produced any particular English version of the Bible. The NRSV's wooden style results in part from its commitment to be as literal as possible. The TEV's meaning-for-meaning approach leads to interpretations such as "making friends" for "reconciliation" that are driven by its commitment to a particular view of understandability. Peterson's rendition of Scripture into everyday speech prizes informality over linguistic precision. In a time when Bible translations proliferate, it is important to know the translation tradition that shapes each version, and to make informed judgments about the tradition in which we choose to stand.

Scripture itself exemplifies the way tradition functions in the life of the community of faith. The English word *tradition* derives from the Latin *traditio* (Greek *paradosis*), which mean "handing over, delivering." Thus Paul, writing to the church in Corinth, says, "For I *handed on* to you as of first importance what I in turn had received" (1 Cor. 15:3), and again, "For I received from the Lord what I also *handed on* to you" (1 Cor. 11:23). What Paul handed on to the Corinthians is also handed on to us every time we confess faith in Christ or celebrate the Lord's Supper. Having received what Paul received and handed on, we too confess faith in the saving significance of Christ's death and resurrection, and we too hand on the "words of institution" that call us to remembrance and hope.

Tradition is ambiguous, however. It is often noted that *traditio* and *paradosis* can be used in two quite different senses. They can mean "handing over" in the sense of passing on beliefs and practices, as in "the faith which was once for all *delivered* to the saints" (Jude 3, RSV). But they can also mean "handing over" in the sense of betraying, as in "Then [Pilate] *handed him over* to them to be crucified" (John 19:16). Beliefs and practices that are handed over to us may enrich us or they may betray us; they may incorporate us into the grace, love, and communion of God, or they may lead us away from the gospel. Thus, while Scripture counsels us to "stand firm and hold fast to the *traditions* that you were taught by us, either by word of mouth or by our letter" (2 Thess. 2:15), it also warns against "making void the word of God through your *tradition* that you have handed on" (Mark 7:13).

The Ambiguity of Tradition

Perhaps tradition's ambiguity is what leads so many Christians to ignore it altogether. Tradition misleads as well as guides, and so we may be tempted to leap over all of the ambiguous norms of faith and life bequeathed to us by our forebears in order to return to "the witness without parallel," Scripture itself. But this is an impossibility. Twenty-first-century Christians have no access to Scripture except via the route laid out by generations of Christians who have read, interpreted, and lived the gospel before us. The route is not always a straight highway. The journey includes detours, twisting paths, wrong turns, and retraced steps. Yet it remains the only route available to us, and we travel it even when we are unaware that we are on a road constructed by our forebears.

It is worth noting that the early Reformers did not bypass or denigrate everything that had preceded them. Calvin in particular thought it was important to stand within the tradition of the church. Frequently and approvingly he quoted the early church fathers— Augustine, Bernard, and others—confident that he was being more faithful to the deep tradition of the church than was the Roman Catholic Church of his day. Calvin had profound respect for all who had labored over the centuries to pass on the faith. His respect for the tradition was not simply historical, however. Calvin believed that he dwelt within the same "one holy catholic and apostolic church" as those who had lived and died the faith before him. He was one with them in the communion of the saints, relating to them with respect and love, and learning from them the shape of faith and faithfulness.

We are not sixteenth-century reformers, but twenty-first-century North Americans whose relationship to tradition is not as positive as Calvin's. With characteristic wit, novelist Gore Vidal observes: "The past for most Americans is a separate universe with its own quaint laws and irrelevant perceptions."[12] Vidal's "most Americans" includes American Christians. Barbara Wheeler, observing trends in North American culture that affect the churches, notes that "we *are more deeply attracted to novelty than tradition*; today, more than ever, we believe that progress, not history, will enrich our lives. As a result, you can sell almost anything in this country if you can convince people that it's not your father's Oldsmobile. . . ."[13]

Most American Christians have scant awareness of and little regard for church tradition. Many think of tradition as an impediment to genuine Christian faith and life. Some imagine that we must shed centuries of doctrinal error and institutional buildup in order to return to the pristine Christian community of the New Testament era. Others imagine that we must shed centuries of racism, patriarchy, and Eurocentrism in order to construct the pristine Christian community of the new era. Both seem to agree that the church's long tradition is a hindrance rather than a help in knowing and living the truth.

We may be able to move beyond careless disregard for tradition with the help of a historian's distinction between tradition and traditional*ism*. "Traditional*ism* is the dead faith of the living," writes Jaroslav Pelikan. "Tradition is the living faith of the dead."[14] "Traditional*ism*" is the uncritical repetition of an accumulated past, while "tradition" is the enduring presence of those who have lived and died the faith before us. When we confess the Apostles' Creed, we acknowledge that we are part of a "communion of saints," a circle of sisters and brothers in the faith who lived their lives within the grace of the Lord Jesus Christ, the love of God, and the communion of the Holy Spirit. Their experience and wisdom are not inferior to our own. We do not stand at the high point of history, looking down upon the inadequate fidelity of all who have preceded us. Taking account of tradition is simply paying heed to our fathers and mothers in the faith. One of our forebears in the faith wryly observed: "Tradition means giving votes to the most obscure of all classes, our ancestors. It is the democracy of the dead. Tradition refuses to submit to the small and arrogant oligarchy of those who happen to be walking about."[15]

There is a danger in any age—not least our own—of arrogance toward those who have preceded us. Perhaps it only seems that our arrogance is particularly disdainful, but our dismissal of the past is not limited to distant centuries. We now exclude Christian thought and life from just a few decades ago. This is what C. S. Lewis called "chronological snobbery, the uncritical acceptance of the intellectual climate common to our own age and the assumption that whatever has gone out of date is on that account discredited."[16] Do we really believe that those who have lived and died the faith before us have nothing to tell us? Do we really think that our ideas and actions are the pinnacle of human achievement, superior to every previous thought?

Recognizing our chronological snobbery may enable us to understand that "our own age is also a 'period,' and certainly has, like all periods, its characteristic illusions. They are likely to lurk in those widespread assumptions which are so ingrained in the age that no one dares to attack or feels it necessary to defend them."[17] Tradition, the living faith of the whole communion of saints, need not be a barrier to the truth about Christian faith and life. Tradition can be liberating, freeing us from captivity to the limited perspective of our own time and place. Without help to recognize the taken-for-granted assumptions of contemporary North America, we become prisoners in the tiny cell of "here and now." Disregarding the church's tradition, out of fear that the past may oppress us, only subjects us to the tyranny of the present.

Suspicious Eyes

Openness to our forebears in the faith can help us overcome our suspicion of tradition and can encourage suspicion of our own age's easy assumptions. Tradition enables us to employ a double suspicion: a humble guardedness about the past *and* a healthy skepticism about the present.

Guardedness about the past opens up an awareness of the cultural particularities of previous historical contexts. As we recognize the ways in which cultural overlays limit the tradition, we may also discover that our unfamiliarity with the past limits our capacity to receive tradition's wisdom. The Second Helvetic Confession (1561) provides a good example of both the limitations and the wisdom of the Reformed tradition that has been handed on to us. In its chapter on baptism, the confession addresses the question of who may baptize: "We teach that baptism should not be administered in the Church by women or midwives. For Paul deprived women of ecclesiastical duties, and baptism has to do with these."[18] Is this simply the product of sixteenth-century patriarchal assumptions, or is something worthwhile going on here? Both.

The second sentence—"For Paul deprived women of ecclesiastical duties, and baptism has to do with these"—uses the Bible inappropriately to confirm a sixteenth-century cultural assumption that women should not participate in any form of church leadership. The first sentence is a different matter, however. In the medieval church, baptisms were performed regularly by midwives or other women attending the birth of a baby. Such midwife baptisms were commonplace, not confined to "emergency baptisms." The Swiss reformers were adamant that baptisms should take place in a church, during regular worship, and that both parents should be present. Baptism was not an inoculation against hell nor was it a private matter. Instead, baptism was a public rite of incorporation into the body of Christ, the church. God's covenant of baptism embraced child, parents, and the congregation in a bond of mutual responsibility. Thus, the Second Helvetic Confession's prohibition of baptisms performed by midwives was an outgrowth of the Reformed churches' recovery of baptism as a sacrament that proclaimed the gospel of grace within worship and embodied the gospel of grace in the ongoing life of the community of faith.

Contemporary Christians are rightly suspicious of tradition's expression of beliefs and practices that excluded women from full participation in the church's life and its ordered ministries. Our reading of Scripture has freed us from many forms of the cultural dispositions that excluded women. Texts such as Galatians 3:27–29 have brought Scripture's critique to bear on traditional church practices: "As many of you as were baptized into Christ have clothed yourselves with Christ. There is no longer Jew or Greek, there is no longer slave or free, there is no longer male and female; for all of you are one in Christ Jesus. And if you belong to Christ, then you are Abraham's offspring, heirs according to the promise." Scripture's critique has opened our eyes to Scripture's own narratives of the leadership of women in the earliest Christian communities, from the women who were the first to proclaim the risen Christ (Luke 24:1–12), to ministers and leaders of house churches known to Paul (Rom. 16:1–16).

The Reformed tradition is in the process of correcting itself on the basis of Scripture's witness. *Sola scriptura*: tradition, including the church's confessional standards, must be measured by the primary standard of Scripture. Thus the Presbyterian Church (U.S.A.)'s most recent confession confirms the full inclusion of women in all "ecclesiastical duties":

> We trust in God the Holy Spirit, . . .
>
> who inspired the prophets and apostles,
>
> rules our faith and life in Christ through Scripture,
>
> engages us through the Word proclaimed,
>
> claims us in the waters of baptism,
>
> feeds us with the bread of life and the cup of salvation,
>
> and calls women and men to all ministries of the Church.[19]

Guardedness about the past, a refusal simply to replicate tradition, can free us from time-bound limitations of thought and action. And yet our guardedness should not lead to smug dismissal of our forebears, thinking of them as hopelessly out of touch with our time. Unlike the Second Helvetic Confession, we are happy to have women pastors baptize our children. However, also unlike the Second Helvetic Confession, we may be happy enough when pastors, women and men, preside at baptisms that are little more than chummy congregational welcomes for the cute babies of charming young families. Contemporary baptisms occur in public worship, but their significance may be as "private" as midwife baptisms in medieval Europe. The tradition's testimony to the ongoing congregational significance of Baptism can engender a healthy suspicion of much contemporary baptismal practice. Have we sentimentalized a powerful proclamation of the gospel and veiled the presence of Christ among us? Does our baptismal practice adequately express testimony to the witness of Scripture?

Do you not know that
all of us who have been baptized into Christ Jesus
were baptized into his death?
Therefore we have been buried with him
by baptism into death,
so that,
just as Christ was raised from the dead
by the glory of the Father,
so we too might walk in newness of life.

(Rom. 6:3–4)

The very differentness of the past can expose the inadequacies of the present. We properly bring suspicion to bear on the past. The early church, the medieval church, the Reformation church, the 1950s church —all were subject to the danger of false consciousness. Thinking themselves faithful, they were often unaware of the infidelities in their belief and practice. Standing outside of their times and places, we are aware of their inadequacies. We can see things they could not or would not see. As we bring the bright beam of suspicion to bear upon the church in other times and places, we can overcome our distance from the past in order to separate the true scandal of the gospel from its cultural overlays. We see the early church's seduction by the privilege and power that came with state sponsorship. We see the medieval church's moral laxity and abuses of popular piety. We see the Reformation churches fragment into rival factions. We see the 1950s church uncritically adopt the mythic values of the cold war. We see all of it, but if this is all we see we have compounded the problem of cultural captivity, not overcome it.

The danger is that as we demystify the cultural categories of the past and suspect the false consciousness of previous generations, we will remain secure in the certitudes of our own culture. We will remain blissfully unaware of our own false consciousness, believing that we modern Christians have developed the correct standards of what is plausible, faithful, historical, believable, and true. As we look back through suspicious eyes, we may assume that we are the arbiters of the false consciousness of others. If we are to escape from surrender to the standards of our own time and place, then, *we* must become the objects of suspicion. Our suspicion of past forms of faith and faithfulness must be accompanied by suspicion of our own forms of faith and faithfulness.

Seventeenth and Twenty-First Centuries in Conversation

Our capacity to suspect our own insights is limited. It is difficult to look honestly at our own time and place, and impossible to transcend it. However, we can be helped by our forebears in the faith. Just as we are suspicious of their temptations to false consciousness, they may be suspicious of us. The tradition of the church may call us into question just as we call it into question. The possibilities of a fruitful conversation with the tradition may be seen in an unlikely place—the seventeenth-century Westminster Standards. The Westminster Confession of Faith, together with the Larger and Shorter Catechisms, strike many contemporary people as unpleasant examples of high Calvinist scholasticism, unsuitable for theological and moral guidance in a time of pluralism, tolerance, and ecumenical sensitivity. Yet Westminster may have some things to say that we need to hear.

During the study period of a session meeting some years ago, I asked the elders to play a word association game. I gave a word, and asked them to call out the first word that came to their minds. The word I gave was *God*. The elders' responses were "love," "Father," "forgiving," "holy," "sovereign," "shepherd," "mercy," "savior," "heaven," "power," "Jesus," "Spirit," and a few others I have forgotten. I then read a selection from Chapter II of the Westminster Confession of Faith: "There is but one only living and true God, who is infinite in being and perfection, a most pure spirit, invisible, without body, parts, or passions, immutable, immense, eternal, incomprehensible, almighty, most wise, most holy, most free, most absolute, working all things according to the counsel of his own immutable and most righteous will, for his own glory. . . ."[20]

The two lists are poles apart in character and content. Even at the few points of overlap the tone is different. The elders' words are warm and tender while Westminster's words are austere and distant. *Our* God is loving and accepting; *their* God is immense and dispassionate. *We* sing, "God of compassion, in mercy befriend us; Giver of grace for our needs all availing, wisdom and strength for each day do Thou send us, patience untiring and courage unfailing," while *their* hymns are mercifully absent from our hymnals. When we read Westminster's abstract words about a distant God, we are grateful that our age has recovered the biblical testimony that "God is love," a generous, welcoming, accepting God who wishes nothing more than our well-being.

If we give Westminster more than a passing glance, we may suspect that crises in England's political and religious life generated the desire for a God who was in control, beyond the reach of warring factions. In a time when internal conflicts threatened to tear the nation apart, when it was uncertain who would rule the church and the state, the men of the Westminster Assembly may have needed a God "most absolute, working all things according to the counsel of his own immutable and most righteous will." Our suspicion is probably well-founded. Westminster's abstractions, often articulated in the negative, seem far removed from the narratives of the God who led Israel from slavery to freedom, sent prophets to call disobedient people home, sent the Son to redeem the world, and the Spirit to be our comforter and advocate. Westminster's need may have led to a false consciousness that deceived rather than revealed.

If we allow Westminster its voice, we may hear it ask us about our need. Is our friendly, all-forgiving deity the whole truth about God? In an age of preoccupation with individual happiness, coupled with personal feelings of insecurity and powerlessness, do we need a God who "likes us just the way we are"? Westminster's suspicions of us may be well-founded. Our God may be too small, far removed from the narratives of the God who gave the Law on Sinai, judged a disobedient people and sent them into exile, suffered death at our hands, and burst upon us in fire and wind. Our need may have led to a false consciousness that deceives rather than reveals.

The point is not to say that Westminster had it right and we have it wrong, any more than to say that our perception is faithful and theirs mistaken. Our conversation with Westminster may enable us to hear the biblical witness more fully, however, and to recover a more complete understanding of God and God's Way in the world. The tradition can provide a needed critique of our own limited faith and life, and open us to a new appreciation of the faith and life that preceded us. We will probably not begin our prayers, "Immense and immutable God, who workest for Thine own glory . . ." but we may be reminded that our God is the "maker of heaven and earth, of all that is, seen and unseen."

Our suspicion of Westminster, and, with its help, our suspicion of ourselves, may open us to a new appreciation of what Westminster was trying to do. My earlier quotation from Chapter 2 stopped too soon. The text continues, ". . . most loving, gracious, merciful, long-suffering, abundant in goodness and truth, forgiving iniquity, transgression, and sin; the rewarder of them that diligently seek him; and withal most just and terrible in his judgments; hating all sin, and who will by no means clear the guilty."[21] The wording seems stilted and we are not prone to speaking of God with long lists of attributes, but it is clear that Westminster was trying, in its own way, to hold together God's majesty and compassion, sovereignty and love, omniscience and patience, holiness and forgiveness. Our seventeenth-century forebears can encourage us to seek the same fullness in our reception of God so that we can avoid imagining a one-sided deity who, like a doting grandfather, forgives everyone of everything all the time.

The Preservation of the Truth

The exhortation to *preserve* the truth may be most pertinent at the point of the church's tradition. Keeping intact the heritage bequeathed to us by our forebears in the faith is difficult, for the temptation to discard the past as an irrelevancy is a clear and present danger. Henry Ford's opinion that "history is more or less bunk" may seem outrageous, yet we commonly dismiss people with the flippant judgment, "You're history," consigning them to the past's "great dust-heap." Preservation of the church's deep tradition is not an antiquarian eccentricity, however, much less a nostalgic preference for a romanticized past. Preserving the tradition may even be seen as an act of *self*-preservation! We conserve the tradition because it gives voice to wisdom that we do not possess, and protects us from the follies that are ours alone.

The church's tradition must never become a museum piece, preserved in a hermetically sealed display case. Our task is not to preserve the tradition, but to preserve the truth. Tradition is an indispensable element in truth's preservation. The tradition divulges insights into the truth that are beyond our experience or understanding. The tradition also challenges our experience and understanding.

In this chapter, and throughout the book, I have quoted sources from the Reformed tradition, particularly John Calvin. I have not done this because the Reformed tradition is the norm of Christian faith and life, or because Calvin is a privileged authority. I quote our forebears in the faith because I have discovered through them angles of vision on the truth of the gospel that I would not have seen on my own. I could cite a number of instances where I think the tradition got it wrong, but my chief interest is discovering the ways that I am led into truth by those who lived and died the faith before me, even dying *for* the faith so that its truth might be preserved for me.

> But we must always give thanks to God for you, brothers and sisters beloved by the Lord, because God chose you as the first fruits for salvation through sanctification by the Spirit and through belief in the truth. For this purpose he called you through our proclamation of the good news, so that you may obtain the glory of our Lord Jesus Christ. So then, brothers and sisters, stand firm and hold fast to the traditions that you were taught by us, either by word of mouth or by our letter.

(2 Thess. 2:13–15)

Notes

1. Milan Kundera, *The Unbearable Lightness of Being* (New York: Harper & Row, 1984), p. 8.
2. "The Ten Theses of Berne," in Arthur C. Cochrane, ed., *Reformed Confessions of the Sixteenth Century* (Louisville: Westminster John Knox Press, 1966/2003), p. 49.
3. Theological Declaration of Barmen, *The Book of Confessions*, 8.11–12.
4. Calvin, *Institutes*, "Subject Matter of the Present Work," p. 6.
5. Ibid., 4.1.9, p. 1023.
6. Confession of 1967, *BC*, 9.02–.03.
7. "The Preface to the Scots Confession of 1560," in Cochrane, ed., *Reformed Confessions*, pp. 164–165.
8. *The French Confession of 1559*, trans. Ellen Babinsky and Joseph D. Small (Louisville: Office of Theology and Worship, 1998), Art. IV, p. 6.
9. "To the Reader," preface to *The Holy Bible: New Revised Standard Version* (Nashville: Thomas Nelson Publishers, 1989), in the first paragraph and in that beginning, "As for the style of English adopted . . . "
10. Preface to the *Good News Bible: Today's English Version* (New York: American Bible Society, 1976).
11. Eugene Peterson, *The Message* (Colorado Springs: NavPress, 1994), p. 7.
12. Gore Vidal, *The Golden Age* (New York: Vintage, 2000), p. 445.
13. Barbara Wheeler, *Who Needs the Church?* (Louisville: Geneva Press, 2004), p. 4.
14. Jaroslav Pelikan, *The Vindication of Tradition* (New Haven, Conn.: Yale University Press, 1984), p. 65.
15. G. K. Chesterton, *Orthodoxy* (New York: Doubleday, 1990), p. 48.
16. C. S. Lewis, *Surprised by Joy* (San Diego: Harcourt Brace Jovanovich, 1955), p. 207.

17. Ibid., p. 208.
18. Second Helvetic Confession, *BC*, 5.191.
19. A Brief Statement of Faith, *BC*, 10.4.
20. Westminster Confession of Faith, *BC*, 6.011.
21. Ibid.

Unity and Diversity

> Later Ellen experienced a religious conversion. She became
> disaffected when the Southern and Northern Presbyterians,
> estranged since the Civil War, reunited after over a hundred
> years. It was not the reunion she objected to, but the liberal
> theology of the Northern Presbyterians, who, according to
> her, were more interested in African revolutionaries than the
> divinity of Christ. She and others pulled out and formed the
> Independent Northlake Presbyterian Church.
>
> Then she became an Episcopalian.
>
> Then suddenly she joined a Pentecostal sect. . . .
>
> I do not know what to make of this.
>
> —Walker Percy, *The Thanatos Syndrome*[1]

The spectrum of American religious life has shattered. From the time
of the nation's colonial beginnings until the recent past, the light of the
gospel was diffracted through the prism of the American experience,
producing distinct bands of recognizable churches: old line Congre-
gationalists, Episcopalians, and Presbyterians; later-arriving Baptists,
Catholics, Lutherans, and Methodists; uniquely American Disciples of
Christ, Holiness churches, and Pentecostals . . . and more. For most of
American history, denominationalism was marked by churches with
distinct identities and internal cohesion spread over a range of Christian
faith and life. The spectrum has shattered. Denominations are now
characterized by internal disparity, disagreement, and division. The
orderly, graded spectrum has been displaced by wildly variegated
kaleidoscopic images *within* each church.

Sexuality issues are the most visible factor in the fragmentation of
church life. Sexual abuse of minors and adults, premarital sex, children
born to unmarried couples and single mothers, abortion, ordination to

ministry of gay and lesbian persons, "gay marriage," a high divorce rate, and other matters related to sex continue to produce deep divisions within Presbyterian, Episcopalian, Catholic, Methodist, and other churches. Sexuality issues are only the most dramatic sources of division within the churches, however. Churches also struggle to cope with internal theological and organizational debates that, while they may result in legislative victories or organizational triumphs for one faction or another, are not resolved in general agreement about the shape of ecclesial faith. Doctrinal disputes seethe within churches ranging from the Southern Baptist Convention to the United Church of Christ. Christology, the authority of Scripture, salvation, and other central elements of Christian faith are battlegrounds rather than common ground. Theological and moral disagreements within the churches are so acute that a particular faction in one church often has more in common with similar factions in other churches than with differing groups within its own church. In the meantime, church members travel easily from one denomination to another, seeking a comfort level that may have more to do with the avoidance of conflict than with its resolution.

Where in all of this is truth? How can the church preserve what it cannot even seem to find? Where is the truth to be found when factions within the churches engage in battles between competing truths?

Diversity

It may be a source of comfort (or despair) to realize that theological and moral diversity is not unique to our time and place. The sixteenth century presents us with an intriguing insight into the relationship between discord and truth:

> We are reproached because there have been manifold dissensions and strife in our churches since they separated themselves from the Church of Rome, and therefore cannot be true churches. . . . We know, to be sure, that the apostle said: "God is not a God of confusion but of peace" (1 Cor. 14:33), and, "While there is jealousy and strife among you, are you not of the flesh?" Yet we cannot deny that God was in the apostolic Church and that it was a true Church, even though there were wranglings and dissensions in it. . . . And there have at all times been great contentions in the Church, and the most excellent teachers of the Church have differed among themselves about important matters without

meanwhile the Church ceasing to be the Church because of these contentions. For thus it pleases God to use the dissensions that arise in the Church to the glory of his name, to illustrate the truth, and in order that those who are in the right might be manifest (1 Cor. 11:19).[2]

The Protestant Reformation led to the breakup of the Great Church, although that was not the Reformers' intention. In response to Catholic criticism of Reformation splits, the Second Helvetic Confession declared that disagreement and conflict were not strangers to the Christian community. More important, the Confession declared that dissension in the church "illustrates the truth," for in the process of debate about differences, the truth will be made manifest. Is this a naive hope? It does not appear that the current internal fragmentation of the contemporary churches will yield the truth anytime soon. Is the Confession's hope an expectation that truth will be manifest only in the long term, following a protracted period of hard debate? Or is truth always plural, never yielding one uniform certainty that is affirmed by all?

The Bible is confessed as "the unique and authoritative witness to Jesus Christ" and "the only infallible guide to faith and practice." Yet the Bible itself is plural rather than uniform, a collection of witnesses and guides. The sixty-six books of the Book are diverse in origin, purpose, content, and expression, yet they are unified in one collection that functions in the church as Scripture. This Scripture functions in the church as canon—the standard of Christian faith and life. Nevertheless, it seems that Scripture can only be understood as *the Scriptures*. The New Testament, a collection of writings composed within a brief span of time, presents us with four Gospels, not one. It offers numerous narratives, letters, tracts, and visions—addressed to different groups of believers in various situations—not one exposition of Christian belief. While the church affirms that these texts are complementary, it remains the case that we are given a diversity of expression, not a unitary one. Imagine how different our understanding of Christian faith would be if the New Testament were confined to Luke, Acts, and Paul's letter to the Philippians.

What unifies the various writings of Scripture, joining them together as canon, is their consistent testimony to God's story with humankind, culminating in the story of Jesus Christ. God's story is told in "many and various ways," however: Leviticus as well as Amos, James as well as Galatians, Ecclesiastes as well as Isaiah, 1 and 2 Timothy as well as 1 and 2 Corinthians, John as well as Mark, and so on. The church affirms all of this as *rich* diversity that deepens our understanding of Christian faith and strengthens our Christian discipleship. Truth is made manifest, not by the clash of competing claims, but by the bonding of complementary apprehensions of a truth that cannot be confined in one simple formulation. The Confession of 1967 expresses the complementary character of truth's fullness as it speaks of God's reconciling act in Jesus Christ and our hope for fulfillment of Christ's rule.

> God's reconciling act in Jesus Christ is a mystery which the Scriptures describe in various ways. It is called the sacrifice of a lamb, a shepherd's life given for his sheep, atonement by a priest; again it is ransom of a slave, payment of debt, vicarious satisfaction of a legal penalty, and victory over the powers of evil. These are an expression of a truth which remains beyond the reach of all theory in the depths of God's love for humankind. They reveal the gravity, cost, and sure achievement of God's reconciling work.[3]

Biblical visions and images of the rule of Christ, such as a heavenly city, the household of God, a new heaven and earth, a marriage feast, and an unending day culminate in the image of the kingdom. The kingdom represents God's triumph over all that resists the divine will and disrupts God's creation.[4]

Scripture expresses the truth of God in Christ in multiple ways, not because Scripture is inconsistent, but because the gospel truth is inexhaustible, resisting all attempts to confine it in a singular formulation. Scriptural diversity is not limitless, however. The New Testament includes Mark, Matthew, Luke, and John, but it excludes the later Gospel of Thomas and the Proto-Gospel of James. The early church winnowed the multiple writings that circulated in the first two centuries, separating those that deepened faith and life from those that narrowed it. The community's winnowing process was not confined to canonical Scripture, for the church also developed the *regula fidei*, the *rule of faith* that summarized the gospel into which people were baptized. As divergent views developed among some groups in the church, the rule of faith was more fully developed in two great creeds of the church—the Nicene Creed and the Apostles' Creed—that said "yes" to some expressions of Christian faith and "no" to divergent views.

The Second Helvetic Confession's confidence may be justified, then. Perhaps dissension does serve to illustrate the truth and manifest those who are in the right. Can we say that the enriching diversity of biblical witness to the truth makes possible the church's separation of truth from error, thus manifesting the truth of Christian faith to all? We do not have to assert the church's unanimous affirmation of perfect truth in order to have confidence in its fidelity to the gospel. Catholic theologian Hans Küng resists all ecclesial claims to infallibility, but he asserts that God preserves the church in the truth in spite of all ever-present and ever-possible errors. "In order to avoid all misunderstandings," says Küng, "it is better to ascribe to the Church, not 'infallibility,' but—on the basis of faith in the promises—indefectibility' or 'perpetuity'; an unshatterability and indestructibility; in brief, a fundamental *remaining* in the truth in spite of all ever possible errors."[5] If the church is not in the truth, which is to say if the church is not in Christ, then it is no longer the church, the body of Christ. But remaining in truth is not dependent on infallible propositions or persons, for it is God who continues his people in constancy, maintaining a faithful witness in the world.

The church's "indefectibility" does not guarantee unanimous acceptance of the whole truth and nothing but the truth. Persons and groups and communities of faith and even denominations within the church may depart from the truth. In certain places or times, parts of the church may be dramatically wrong about foundational matters of faith and life. Thus, although we can be confident that God keeps promises and that the one holy catholic apostolic church will be kept in the truth, we must still deal with our own specific context, striving to preserve ourselves in the truth. It seems that the Second Helvetic Confession is fundamentally right, in the long term, but this does not assure us that the truth will become manifest through our particular dissensions.

Celebrating Diversity

North American mainline church life is now characterized by a plurality that is neither Scripture-like complementarity nor the limited diversity that winnows truth from error. The churches seem to have adopted pluralism as an essential tenet, with "celebrating diversity" as its liturgical component. Pluralism and diversity are not only acknowledged, but also prized as positive values that enrich the community of faith. The Presbyterian Church (U.S.A.)'s *Book of Order* devotes a section in its chapter on "The Church and Its Unity" to "Diversity and Inclusiveness." Thus, in affirming the unity of the church as a gift of its Lord, the church's constitution stipulates that the PC(USA) "shall give full expression to the rich diversity within its membership and shall provide means which will assure a greater inclusiveness leading to wholeness in its emerging life." Lest the point be missed, the *Book of Order* enumerates groups that are included in the church's diversity: "Persons of all racial ethnic groups, different ages, both sexes, various disabilities, diverse geographical areas, different theological positions consistent with the Reformed tradition, as well as different marital conditions (married, single, widowed, or divorced)."[6]

Who could argue against the necessity of including all of God's people in the life of God's church? Yet it was not that long ago that church leadership was limited to white men. The church's current commitment to the full inclusion of women, people of color, young people, and other enumerated groups is a mandate of the gospel, not merely a concession to the bourgeois ethic of inclusivity. This gospel mandate is at the heart of the New Testament. Bringing Jews and Gentiles together in the body of Christ is a foundational biblical paradigm for the Christian refusal to exclude groups of people: "But now in Christ Jesus you who once were far off have been brought near in the blood of Christ. For he is our peace, who has made us both one, and has broken down the dividing wall of hostility, . . . that he might create in himself one new humanity in place of the two, so making peace, and might reconcile us both to God in one body through the cross, thereby bringing the hostility to an end" (Eph. 2:13–16, RSV alt.). Racial hostility, sex discrimination, dismissal of youth, prejudice against persons with disabilities . . . all are ruled out by the good news of Christ. The only objection some raise to the *Book of Order*'s list is that it ought to be lengthened, adding other categories of persons to be guaranteed full access within the church's life.

The contemporary celebration of diversity goes beyond the inclusion of all believers in the community of faith, however. Rather than emphasizing the incorporation of all persons in the body of Christ, the current celebration of diversity highlights the various experiences, insights, and gifts that each group and each person brings to the whole. But this wholesale approval of diverse experiences leads, ironically, to partitions within the church. Celebrating each experience may construct enclaves of privileged experience that are home to particular groups while barring entrance to others. The American version of pluralism has tended to transform loose communities of natural affinity into self-contained pockets of experience that are inaccessible to those who do not share the experience.

Spawned by pluralism, clusters of closed experience encourage distinctions. Formed as cohesive communities of experience and conviction, they become mutually exclusive and so lead to fragmentation. Women's experience . . . born again experience . . . the experience of inherited power . . . black experience . . . the experience of youth . . . new immigrants' experience . . . the experience of the poor . . . gay and lesbian experience . . . the experience of boomers, X-ers, busters, and other sociologists' fantasies . . . all are presented as normative experience *for those who share the experience.* To the extent that these pockets of experience are unavailable to "outsiders," and both advocacy and critique are restricted to "insiders," the church becomes balkanized (and sometimes ideological cleansing becomes the order of the day). Pockets of experience easily become pockets of "truth": women's truth, the truth of the young, black truth, white truth, and on and on. Since each "community of truth" possesses truthfulness that is unavailable to others, the best that can be hoped for is a smorgasbord of truths from which all can sample foreign dishes whose ingredients are unknown and unknowable.

The Body of Christ

Is there an alternative to the pluralism of separated experiences, insights, and gifts? Surely the church should not strive for uniformity that suppresses diversity. Too often in the church's life, an emphasis on unity has imposed the uniformity of the powerful, stifling different voices and diminishing varied insights. The available options are not limited to insular pluralities and oppressive uniformity, however. Embedded in the New Testament is a way of understanding the community of faith that values both the church's unity and its diversity, and appreciates the relationship between them.

The "body of Christ" texts—1 Corinthians 12, Romans 12, Ephesians 1 and 4, and Colossians 1—provide angles of vision on the life of the contemporary church that enable us to see ourselves afresh. Each text, in ways familiar to most Christians, portrays the church as the body of Christ. Our very familiarity with "body of Christ" may be a problem, however, for our long acquaintance may diminish its capacity to inform our understanding. We have heard it so often, in classes and sermons and meetings, that we think we have heard it all. The Bible's shocking metaphor, "body of Christ," has become a cliché.

"Human organizations are like the human body" is a modern truism. The comparison is embedded in everyday references to "the body politic," "a body of troops," and "legislative bodies," as well as less obvious allusions to "corporate life." Unfortunately, conventional use of the organization-body figure of speech shapes the way New Testament "body of Christ" texts are understood in the church. "Each of us has something to contribute to the whole church (so the story goes). The church would be incomplete without the diverse gifts of its members, and none of the members can go it alone." Whether in its congregational form (singers, organizers, educators, kitchen workers, and caregivers are all needed to make church life whole) or its denominational form (liberals, conservatives, evangelists, social activists, racial ethnic groups, bureaucrats, and pastors need each other in order to be complete), the comparison of the church to the body is commonplace.

Correlation between an organization and the human body is not only a modern platitude. It was already a cliché in the first century. The human organization as body was a well-known Hellenistic figure of speech used to describe the city-state, the family, armies, and other institutions and associations.[7] If Paul had only been noting that diverse persons and groups in the church function together as a unified whole, the readers of his letters might have dismissed it as a truism. Comparing any organization, even the church, to the human body was little more than first-century conventional wisdom. But Paul was not being trite.

When we look closely at the "body of Christ" passages in 1 Corinthians, Romans, Ephesians, and Colossians, we quickly move beyond predictable understanding. The texts do far more than compare the human organization—church—to the one, yet differentiated, human organism—body. Rather than saying simply that the church is *like* the body, Paul makes the startling claim that the church *is* the body *of Christ*. It is as the body *of Christ* that the church is one, and it is as the body *of Christ* that the church's diversity is experienced.

> For just as the body is one and has many members, and
> all the members of the body, though many, are one body,
> *so it is with Christ.* . . . Now you are the body *of Christ* and
> individually members of it. (1 Cor. 12:12, 27)

> For as in one body we have many members, and not all
> the members have the same function, so we, who are
> many, are one body *in Christ*, and individually we are
> members one of another. (Rom. 12:4–5)

> [God] has put all things under [Christ's] feet and has made
> him the head over all things for the church, which is *his*
> body, the fullness of him who fills all in all. (Eph. 1:22–23)
> There is one body and one Spirit, just as you were called
> to the one hope of your calling, one Lord, one faith, one
> baptism, one God and Father of all, who is above all and

through all and in all. . . . We must grow up in every way
into *him who is the head*, into *Christ*, from whom the
whole body, joined and knit together by every ligament
with which it is equipped, as each part is working properly,
promotes the body's growth in building itself up in love.
(Eph. 4:4–6, 15–16)

[Christ] himself is before all things, and in him all things
hold together. *He is the head* of the body, the church; he
is the beginning, the firstborn from the dead, so that he
might come to have first place in everything. . . . I am now
rejoicing in my sufferings for your sake, and in my flesh I
am completing what is lacking in Christ's afflictions for the
sake of *his* body, that is, the church. (Col. 1:17–18, 24)

The jarring element in these texts is not "the church is like the
body," but rather, "the church-body is the body *of Christ*, the body *in
Christ*, the body whose *head is Christ*"! The church-body is not its own
body, but the body of *Christ*; and the body of Christ is not only Christ's
body, but also *the church*! Clearly, Paul's language is not a mere simile,
but a rich metaphor in which two disparate terms—church-body and
Christ-body—are brought together in a way that discloses an altogether
new reality. Church-body and Christ-body are each intelligible separately,
but *church-body-of-Christ* stretches language to the breaking point in
order to create a new apprehension of truth.

The church is not its own. It is not self-generated or self-directed.
It is not master of its own life, able to determine its own nature or
purpose. The church is not its own, for it belongs to another, to Christ,
precisely as Christ's body. The church belongs to Christ alone, and yet
the bond of *church* and *body of Christ* is not a natural one; a distinction
remains. Neither is collapsed into the other, as if the church were the
continuing form of Christ's earthly presence, or as if the real church
dwells in Christ's heavenly presence. Rather, *as the body of Christ* the
church exists as a visible collection of ordinary people that is nothing
less than the locus of the real presence of Christ.

It is not mere coincidence that the other striking New Testament
use of "body of Christ" also discloses Christ's real presence. "This
[bread] is my body," says Jesus, bidding his disciples to take, eat, and
remember him. Bread is Christ's body. Church is Christ's body. Bread

remains ordinary bread and church remains an ordinary human community, yet both bread and church are the locus of Christ's presence. "Jesus Christ gives us in the Supper the real substance of his body and blood," says Calvin, "so that we may possess him fully, and, possessing him, have part in all his blessings."[8] Christ's real presence in eucharistic bread and wine nourishes the body of Christ, constituting and manifesting the real presence of Christ in the church.

As if all this were not enough, the texts suggest that we are Christ's *wounded* body, even Christ's *crucified* body. The suffering, executed, dead, and buried Jesus has been raised to new life of course, but resurrection does not eradicate crucifixion. It is the crucified one who is raised, and the resurrected one is none other than the crucified. As the body of *Christ* the church is not a triumphant, glorified body. Each time we come together to eat the bread and drink the wine of communion with Christ we proclaim the Lord's *death* until he comes. The church that gives eucharistic thanks for communion in the body and blood of Christ is the body of the crucified-risen Christ. Like its crucified and risen Lord, the church lives with nail marks in its hands and a gash in its side (John 20:24–29), as a slaughtered lamb (Rev. 5:6), as the body whose hands and feet remain pierced (Luke 24:36–40).

The church is known as the wounded body of Christ in the letters to Corinth, Rome, Ephesus, and Colossae. Paul's "body of Christ" passages neither celebrate the church's diversity nor applaud its unity. Surprisingly, he employs the stunning image in contexts of discord and division, not peace and harmony. It is also surprising to realize that discord in the community of faith is sometimes attributed to excessive celebration of the diverse gifts given by the Spirit! Each diverse gift, celebrated apart from other gifts, led to self-satisfaction, pride, detachment, and quarrels. Yes, there are varieties of gifts, but there is one Spirit; varieties of service, but one Lord; varieties of working, but one God. Diversity is not given for its own sake, but for the sake of the common good. Paul draws on "body of Christ" when pride and self-sufficiency threaten to create separation and dissension, urging unity because Christ's body should not be divided. The opening of 1 Corinthians is typical: "Now I appeal to you, brothers and sisters, by the name of our Lord Jesus Christ, that all of you be in agreement and that there be no divisions among you, but that you be united in the same mind and the same purpose" (1 Cor. 1:10). Yet the unity Paul urges is a unity *of* diverse members, not a unity imposed *over* diverse members: "For as in one body we have many members, and all the members do not have the same function, so we, though many, are one body in

Christ, and individually members one of another. Having gifts that differ according to the grace given to us, let us use them" (Rom. 12:4–6, RSV).

The body of Christ appears in Ephesians at the climax of a remarkable section of the letter, Ephesians 4:1—5:2. The apostle begs the community to live a life worthy of its calling, bearing with one another in love and maintaining unity in the bonds of peace. The passage continues with an interplay of the words *one*, *all*, and *some*. Paul says there is . . .

> **one** body **one** Spirit **one** hope **one** Lord **one** faith
> **one** baptism **one** God and Father
> of **all** above **all** through **all** in **all**
> **some** apostles **some** prophets **some** evangelists
> **some** pastors and teachers

This intricate passage proclaims that in our life together as the church, we are *one* body, called by the *one* Spirit to share *one* hope. Our *one* faith is trust in the *one* Lord to whom we are bound in our *one* baptism. This reveals the gracious love of the *one* God and Father of us *all*, who dwells above *all*, yet lives in *all* and works through *all*. However, the one triune God who draws us all together does not formulate a homogenous community of standardized faith and life. On the contrary, the one God creates a variegated community by giving a variety of gifts. In our Ephesians text, the gifts he gives are that *some* are apostles, *some* prophets, *some* evangelists, and *some* pastors and teachers.

The gifts enumerated in Ephesians have a purpose. Apostles, prophets, evangelists, and pastor-teachers are God's gifts to equip all the saints for the work of ministry and for building up the body of Christ. Other "body of Christ" texts—Romans 12 and 1 Corinthians 12 in particular—include different lists of gifts that are given to the community, but the purpose of gifts is the same—building up the body so that it can fulfill its calling. In Romans, prophecy, ministry, teaching, exhorting, giving, leading, and showing compassion are both the gifts God has given and the work the body is given to do. In 1 Corinthians, various ministries require multiple gifts that are given "for the common good." The lists are different because they are not intended to set forth a standard catalog of the only gifts God gives. Various lists occur in particular contexts, demonstrating the lavish grace of God and the ways in which the gifts work together to nourish the body for its mission and ministries.

Gift and Calling

Scripture calls the body of Christ to live as a unified whole in the harmonious interplay of its indispensable parts precisely because that is *not* the way it does live. "Body of Christ" is not a hackneyed convention to be trotted out in honor of the church's unity or to celebrate its complementary multiplicity. Rather, "Body of Christ" is a disturbing rebuke to the church's self-inflicted wounds of division: division among denominations, within denominations, and in congregations.

The *unity* of the church is our calling, but never our achievement. The church's unity is gift before it is calling, and the call proceeds from the gift. The texts are clear that our embodiment in Christ is a given: "We, who are many, *are* one body in Christ" (Rom. 12:5); "now you *are* the body of Christ" (1 Cor. 12:27); "There *is* one body and one Spirit" (Eph. 4:4). We are not called to strive for the achievement of equilibrium or uniformity because the church's unity is a gift of its Lord. We may squander our inheritance or bury our gift, but the church's foundational reality is the oneness of the people of God, the identity of the body of Christ, the integrity of the temple of the Holy Spirit. We are one with another whether we like it or not. In the midst of all of our differences and disagreements, we *are* one body *in Christ*.

Unity, then, is not an accomplishment. The church cannot create, legislate, or command unity. Our oneness is grounded in "the unity of the Spirit," not the unity of *The Book of Confessions*, much less the *Book of Order*. But the Spirit's gift is also the church's calling. The community can never be content with its fragmentation or satisfied with an invisible "spiritual" unity. "If then, there is any encouragement in Christ," says Paul, "any consolation from love, any sharing in the Spirit, any compassion and sympathy, make my joy complete: be of the same mind, having the same love, being in full accord and of one mind" (Phil. 2:1–2).

It is also true that the *diversity* of the church is not our achievement or the natural by-product of our innate multiplicity. The church's diversity grows from the generosity of the gifts given by the triune God: Spirit (1 Corinthians), God (Romans), and Christ (Ephesians). Because the church's variety is not our doing, we are not called to manufacture or to brandish our diversity. We may idolize our gifts or isolate our endowments, but the church's foundational reality is the richly gifted multiplicity of the one people of God, the one body of Christ, the one temple of the Holy Spirit.

Diversity is not a capability and the church is not simply a mosaic of natural human variety. Our diversity grows from "manifestations of the Spirit," not from an assortment of abilities and talents, much less from the characteristics of rights-based constituencies. The Spirit's gifts are also the church's calling, however: The community can never be content with patterns of cultural conformity or satisfied with neglecting or excluding any of the Spirit's gifts. "Having gifts that differ according to the grace given to us," says Paul, "let us use them" (Rom. 12:6, RSV).

A striking feature of the "body of Christ" texts is that unity and diversity are not seen as mutually exclusive alternatives, but as intimately related, mutually indispensable aspects of an organic whole. The unity of the church cannot be conceived apart from the variety of gifts that flourish within the whole. Diversity in the church makes no sense apart from the life-giving unity of the whole. The unity of the body is comprised by the variety of gifts, and the variety of gifts compose the whole.

Apart from diversity, the church's unity would quickly degenerate into uniformity. Apart from unity, the church's diversity would quickly fragment in disarray. What may be less apparent is that attempts to achieve uniformity are a clear and present threat to unity as well. Without variety, the church ceases to be a living body, much less the body of Christ. What may also be less apparent is that indiscriminate variation is destructive of diversity. Without unity, the church ceases to be a body at all, and surely not the body of Christ.

Truth and Love

Our Ephesians text (one–all–some) advances to the proclamation that Christ's gifts are given to equip us for the work of ministry, for building up the body of Christ. But Paul does not stop there. Building up the body of Christ has a goal in view:

> . . . until all of us come to the unity of the faith and of the knowledge of the Son of God, to maturity, to the measure of the full stature of Christ. We must no longer be children, tossed to and fro and blown about by every wind of doctrine. . . . But speaking the truth in love, we must grow up in every way into him who is the head, into Christ, from whom the whole body, joined and knit together by every ligament with which it is equipped, as each part is working properly, promotes the body's growth in building itself up in love. (Eph. 4:13–16)

The mature, strong body of Christ is unified in faith, resistant to the illnesses of false doctrine, able to know and speak the truth. The text then goes on to proclaim that the life of the body of Christ is new life. The old life of false beliefs and false living must be abandoned, because "That is not the way you learned Christ! For surely you have heard about him and were taught in him, as truth is in Jesus" (Eph. 4:20–21). We are all, together, to put away falsehood and "speak the truth to our neighbors, for we are members of one another" (4:25).

Life as the body of Christ, our life together as a community of faith, is a life aimed at knowing, speaking, and living the truth. The Greek word *aletheuo*, translated in the NRSV as "speak(ing) the truth" in 4:15 and 4:25, is a richer and more comprehensive term than straightforward verbal communication. *Aletheuo* includes truthful speaking, but only as part of a larger way of living that encompasses cherishing, maintaining, and doing the truth. Other English translations render the word in more inclusive ways: "maintain the truth" (Revised English Bible), "hold firmly to the truth" (Phillips), and "live by the truth" (Jerusalem Bible). Perhaps we can capture the term's breadth by rendering it as "be truthful," that is, embody the truth of the gospel in thought, word, and deed. "Being truthful (cherishing, speaking, and living the truth) in love, we must grow up in every way into him who is the head, into Christ" and "Let us all be truthful (cherish, speak, and live the truth) with our neighbors, for we are members of one another." We are not joined together as a collection of different conceptual truths, much less competing verbal truths, even less dueling truths. A grown-up body of believers cherishes the Truth that is Jesus Christ together, maintains the truth about Jesus Christ together, speaks the truth of the gospel of Jesus Christ together, and lives in the truth of Jesus Christ together.

The church's great purpose of preserving the truth is not merely getting our doctrine straight, although it includes getting our doctrine straight. Theology is essential because what we believe and how we live are intimately connected. Among the "Historic Principles" that have been in the Presbyterian Church (U.S.A.)'s constitution since 1788 is the conviction that "no opinion can be either more pernicious or more absurd than that which brings truth and falsehood upon a level, and represents it as of no consequence what a man's opinions are. On the contrary, we are persuaded that there is an inseparable connection between faith and practice, truth and duty. Otherwise, it would be of no consequence either to discover truth or to embrace it."[9] Living the truth depends on knowing the truth. Knowing the truth does not assume unanimity in all things, of course. Christians can and do differ about matters of faith and life. What Christians cannot differ about is the mutual commitment to seek, discover, and embrace the truth together.

Love is indispensable to the search for truth. Throughout the New Testament, unity in Christ is understood as the harmony of love. The "body of Christ" passages climax in exhortations to love: "Let love be genuine . . .; love one another with mutual affection" (Rom. 12:9–10). "But strive for the greater gifts. And I will show you a still more excellent way. . . . And the greatest of these is love" (1 Cor. 12:31; 13:13). "And live in love, as Christ loved us" (Eph. 5:1). The church's union with Christ and its unity in Christ is—fundamentally and ultimately—communion in love. At its heart, preservation of the truth is dependent on the preservation of love within the church.

Communion in love is the way of life for a church that knows the Truth and seeks the truth about the Truth. Does this communion in love characterize the life of American churches today? Or is communion in love broken as interdenominational divisions deteriorate into intradenominational chaos and interpersonal hostility? The fractured reality of the church's life is all too apparent. The Bible assumes and urges a different reality. "Beloved, let us love one another, because love is from God; everyone who loves is born of God and knows God. . . . Beloved, since God loved us so much, we also ought to love one another. . . . The commandment we have from him is this: those who love God must love their brothers and sisters also" (1 John 4:7, 11, 21). Throughout the New Testament we find exhortations to a communion of love, for the Truth lives in love, and the truth about the gospel of Truth is only preserved in love. Within our churches, bonds of communion are too easily broken in battles over truth that yield, as first casualties, love and truth itself. Within the faithful communion of the church, love bears all things, trusts all things, hopes all things, endures all things.

One last look at Ephesians 4 may serve as a benediction at the conclusion of this exploration of truth's preservation. Paul begins this section of his letter with a plea to his readers—including his twenty-first-century readers: "I . . . beg you to lead a life worthy of the calling to which you have been called, with all humility and gentleness, with patience, bearing with one another in love, making every effort to maintain the unity of the Spirit in the bond of peace" (4:1–3). Preserving the truth is integral to our calling. In congregations, denominations, and the church catholic, we are called to seek, learn, share, and live the truth of the gospel. Too often, preservation of the truth takes the form of defensive battles against others, as if the calling were to preserve *our* truth over against the so-called "truth" of others. Making "truth" a fortress against others is not worthy of our calling.

- A life worthy of our calling is lived with humility: "For by the grace given to me I say to everyone among you [every person, interest group, faction, denomination] not to think of yourself more highly than you ought to think, but to think with sober judgment, each according to the measure of faith that God has assigned. . . . [For we] are one body in Christ, and individually we are members one of another" (Rom. 12:3, 5).

- A life worthy of our calling is lived with gentleness and meekness: "You must understand this, my beloved: let everyone be quick to listen, slow to speak, slow to anger; for your anger does not produce God's righteousness. Therefore . . . welcome with meekness the implanted word that has the power to save your souls" (James 1:19–21).
- A life worthy of our calling is lived with patience: "Love is patient; love is kind; love is not envious or boastful or arrogant or rude. It does not insist on its own way" (1 Cor. 13:4–5).
- A life worthy of our calling is lived by bearing with one another in love: "Bear with one another and, if one has a complaint against another, forgive each other; just as the Lord has forgiven you, so you also must forgive" (Col. 3:13).
- A life worthy of our calling makes every effort to maintain the unity of the Spirit in the bonds of peace: "Finally, all of you, have unity of spirit, sympathy, love for one another, a tender heart, and a humble mind. . . . It is for this that you were called" (1 Peter 3:8–9).

Let anyone who has an ear
listen to what the Spirit is saying to the churches

Grace, mercy, and peace will be with us
from God the Father and from Jesus Christ, the Father's Son
in truth and love

Notes

1. Walker Percy, *The Thanatos Syndrome* (New York: Farrar, Straus, Giroux, 1987) p. 353.
2. Second Helvetic Confession, *The Book of Confessions*, 5.133.
3. Confession of 1967, *BC*, 9.09.
4. Ibid., 9.54.
5. Hans Küng, *Infallible? An Inquiry* (Garden City, N.Y.: Doubleday, 1971), p. 185.
6. *Book of Order*, G-4.0403.
7. *Theological Dictionary of the New Testament*, vol. 7, ed. Gerhard Kittel and Gerhard Friedrich (Grand Rapids: Eerdmans, 1971), pp. 1038–1039, 1041. See also J. A. T. Robinson, *The Body, Studies in Biblical Theology*, no. 5 (London: SCM Press, 1952), pp. 159–160.
8. John Calvin, *Short Treatise on the Holy Supper of Our Lord*, in *Calvin: Theological Treatises*, ed. J. K. S. Reid (Philadelphia: Westminster Press, 1954), p. 148.
9. *Book of Order*, G-1.0304.

9

Study Questions

Introduction

1. Have you heard of the Great Ends of the Church?

2. Is your faith community guided by the Great Ends? Does it pay attention to some Ends more than others?

3. God is neither male nor female; God is personal yet beyond gender. Yet historically most language referring to God has employed male pronouns. Small confesses that he does not know a good solution to the problem of expressing God as personally engaged with the world without using gendered language. How does your congregation prefer to talk about God?

Chapter 1

1. How would you answer a stranger who stopped you on the street and asked, "what is truth?" How would you answer a good friend? your child? Would the answers be different?

2. God created the world as a place filled with many forms of life. Over the course of time, nations of diverse peoples have grown up throughout the world, with different customs and languages. Human diversity has become increasingly apparent, as our world has "grown smaller" because of sophisticated forms of transportation and communication. Is there still *one* truth? Can you assume that your truth is another person's truth?

3. Authority is questioned today more than it was, say, fifty years ago. What problems does this situation introduce? What benefits?

4. Does the church have authority to speak to social issues?

5. Think of an issue that has been framed by the value of individual choice. How has individualism, valuing individual responsibility and the right of individual freedom, replaced the notion of a respected collective authority in your community?

6. Discuss the situation that Small recounts of the worship team at a national conference on pages 10–11. Do you agree that we should not have to profess faith statements claimed by our tradition if they contradict personal belief? Why or why not?

7. "Truth is the shape of our relationship with God through Christ in the power of the Holy Spirit" (page 13). Truth is Christ, and the church is called to preserve the Truth. Small continues by saying that we need to discern the distinction between idolatry and faithfulness to the gospel in our daily lives and to be alert to idolatry's challenge to Truth. How might we go about distinguishing forms of idolatry and Truth, which we are called to preserve?

Chapter 2

1. Small states: "The church's urgent task is always to test its preferred 'Jesus' by the accounts of the Gospels and other New Testament writings" (p. 22). What are some examples of a "preferred Jesus"? How can your faith community avoid constructing such a Jesus?

2. The Gospels tell the story of Jesus, but "they are not histories of his life and death. Instead, *the* Gospels are proclamations of *the* gospel, presentations of the good news of God's salvation for all people . . ." (p. 22). What is the difference between proclamation and telling a story, or relating history?

3. Without a relationship of trust and loyalty to Christ, belief is lifeless. Explain the difference between believing that something is true and having faith in something. Do your beliefs make a difference in your decisions about how you live?

4. It is impossible *not* to respond to Jesus' call to follow him—either one says yes, no, or maybe. But the way itself is not always clear. Why do you think this is?

5. What does Small warn against when he says, "Jesus is not a confirmation of human aspirations, but the one whose words and deeds proclaim something radically new, often in the face of human aspirations" (p. 28)?

6. What is the danger of splitting our understanding of Jesus Christ into the Jesus of the Gospels and the risen Christ of the New Testament letters? Why has it always been important to keep the two aspects together?

7. Imagine looking into the face of Jesus Christ. What do you see? What feelings does this evoke? What thoughts arise in response? To what does the Truth of Christ call you?

Chapter 3

1. If God is love, what does love look like? How is this different from saying that we see God when we see love?

2. "God's involvement is so active, so intimate, that who God is becomes fully known in and through Jesus Christ. In this recognition lies the genesis of what has come to be known as the doctrine of the Trinity" (p. 35). Does your church pay much attention to the Trinity? If not, is one Person—Father, Son, or Holy Spirit—worshiped more than the others? What are some of the reasons that your church might have for avoiding discussion of one or more of the Persons?

3. Small states in reference to understanding God: "Shared clarity is not a certain outcome, . . . for while inevitable differences of interpretation can be mutually enriching, they can also be divisive and even destructive. Sometimes interpretations are so divergent that the church must make a fundamental decision between starkly opposing versions of the faith, between orthodoxy and heresy, between right worship and wrong choice. . . . The Trinity is the church's shared clarification of God's self-disclosure, God's freely communicated self-revelation in the person of Christ and the activity of the Spirit" (p. 44). From pages 44–50, construct in your own words a defense for retaining the classical Trinitarian understanding of God.

4. Discuss the relationship of the church in formation and the triune God. How did the Rule of Faith function to unite the church?

5. What was at stake in the issue of the full divinity of Son and Spirit with the Father?

Chapter 4

1. What are some of the challenges to Christianity's truths? Do you believe that anything challenges Christianity's Truth?

2. How do you think the church should respond to issues such as abortion and gay rights: Should it stay away from them or address them in a certain way? Should the church stay out of politics?

3. Do the great world religions offer the same truth? Why is religious pluralism such an important issue for Christian communities?

4. Paul warned the Galatians against falling prey to the lures of mystery cults. Are similar types of temptations present today? If so, how? What forms might these enticements take? How are they enslaving?

5. On page 63 Small refers to the theological statement affirmed by the 2002 General Assembly, *Hope in the Lord Jesus Christ*. He notes that "Jesus Christ is the Way" is "in the first instance, God's Way to us, and then God's Way with us, and only then our way to God." Why is this order important? How is truth freeing? In what way is it empowering?

6. How would you answer another Christian who asked you, "Who can be saved?" How would you answer a person of another faith?

Chapter 5

1. How would you describe the relationship between your faith community and the ideal church?

2. Small notes that one of the worshiping assembly's primary tasks is to preserve the gospel's truth by proclaiming it. What difference would it make in your congregation if, before each session meeting and every committee meeting, this question were asked: "When the congregation assembles for worship on the Lord's Day and at other times during the week, is the word of God purely preached and heard, and are the sacraments purely celebrated according to Christ's institution?" (p. 74).

3. If our standard is Jesus Christ, the Icon of God, what are two measurements provided through worship that show us what this standard looks like? How does your church use this standard to guide its life?

4. Is celebration of the Lord's Supper central to your congregational life? What difference does this make for your own sense of God's power and presence throughout the week?

5. How is baptism practiced in your congregation? Is it an office that functions "to offer and set forth Christ to us, and in him the treasures of heavenly grace"? (Calvin, *Institutes* 4.14.17.)

6. Imagine that preaching is the very giving and receiving of the Word in Jesus Christ, which makes Christ actually present to those present. This is, in fact, the Reformed understanding of preaching. Note that receiving the Word is part of the process. Thus, the Spirit is not only present in the preacher's speech; it is also very much active in the hearing. If you take this seriously, what difference might this make in the way you experience both worship and your life in between sermons?

7. Have you noticed the ways that your church is related to other churches in your area through the presbytery? Has your presbytery ever become involved in conflictual situations that have required a third party's mediating role in your faith community (or in others)? If so, what was this like?

Chapter 6

1. Liturgists and preachers often follow the reading of Scripture with the phrase, "The word of God." The people reply, "Thanks be to God!" Small states, "There is no doubt that Scripture is the polestar that keeps the church on course, guiding its faith and faithfulness" (p. 83) How do you think that this applies to the life of your faith community? What about the PC(USA)?

2. What do you notice about the confessional excerpts on pages 83–84? Do they express Scripture's actual function in the church today? Why or why not?

3. How often do you study Scripture? Do you usually read Scripture alone? in study groups? in worship? What is the difference between corporate and individual study?

4. How do you prepare yourself for reading Scripture? Do you think your life would be different if you studied Scripture more often?

5. Scripture helps us "to see God more plainly, to perceive ourselves more honestly, to view the world more fully, to pay closer attention to the paths laid out in front of us" (p. 90). Why, then, do we tend to avoid using this aid, these corrective lenses, as John Calvin called Scripture, as often as we might?

6. What does Small mean when he condemns as barren those views that dismiss Scripture as myth or reject it because it seems to denigrate women or lift up the powerful (pp. 93–99)? How is it possible to transcend one's worldview when reading Scripture? How do you make the transition between the world of Scripture and that of your culture?

Chapter 7

1. What value do you place on the Reformed tradition? Do you know much about it?

2. The Reformed church today says about itself that it is "Reformed and always being reformed" by the Word of God. Sometimes this statement is abbreviated to "Reformed and always reforming." How does this change the meaning? Why is the first statement the accurate expression?

3. Small reminds us that the community of faith is the creation of the Word of God, and, by extension, so is the tradition that belongs to it. How do you see this heritage in your community of faith?

4. With which Bible translations are you familiar? Which one or ones do you prefer?

5. Do you find Jaroslav Pelikan's distinction between "tradition" and "traditionalism," which Small cites on p. 104, helpful when talking about the history of the church? Why or why not?

6. Do you agree that this generation is particularly disdainful of things of the past? Why do you think this is?

7. How might conversation with a confession from an earlier era, such as the Westminster or the Second Helvetic, adjust some of the "wayward" theological assumptions that are characteristic of today's culture?

Chapter 8

1. How diverse is your congregation? Are you aware of diversity in your denomination as a whole? What are some of the forms diversity takes?

2. How do you think that the church could become more diverse? How would this be a good thing? What would be the challenges?

3. Why do you think that within the body of Christ, which professes the same faith, there are opposing interpretations of important doctrinal issues—and factions formed around them?

4. How does your community of faith deal with conflict? Do you think that conflict is healthy or problematic? Why?

5. The New Testament portrays a community of faith that valued both diversity and unity and strove to nurture each. This called for a particular relationship between the two. The metaphor "body of Christ" has become a cliché today. Look at the texts 1 Corinthians 12, Romans 12, Ephesians 1 and 4, and Colossians 1. What is particular about the way in which the body of Christ is portrayed?

6. Small says that love is essential to the preservation of the truth. "Communion in love is the way of life for a church that knows the Truth and seeks the truth about the Truth" (p. 127). This preservation of the Truth is not the same as building a fortress around our beliefs. Rather, it means relating to others whose understanding differs from ours through the Spirit of love. Thus, peace is not an effort of our own creation but a gift. Imagine the way that your denomination would operate if it were truly to live by the love of the Spirit.